GOOD HOUSEKEEPING

SIMPLE HOUSEHOLD WISDOM

GOOD HOUSEKEEPING

SIMPLE HOUSEHOLD WISDOM

425 EASY WAYS TO CLEAN & ORGANIZE YOUR HOME

EDITED BY SARA LYLE BOW

HEARST books

CONTENTS

WELCOME!

I grew up in a DIY household—both my parents are wizards at fixing and making things. By the time they sent me out into the world, I'd learned to frame a wall, sew, bake bread, quilt, hang wallpaper and drill a hole, among other household tasks. Pushing me to learn these things was one of the greatest gifts they ever gave me. Today I know that no matter what happens, I can rely on myself to get things done.

That's how I'd like you to feel when reading *Good Housekeeping Simple Household Wisdom*. We've taken 130 years of tips, tricks and advice—and created this go-to guide that will help you make every day a little easier, a little more organized and a lot more fun. Plus we've tapped the Good Housekeeping Institute experts for top-tested products, time-saving solutions, easy how-tos and the GH Seal Holders you need to know about.

The book opens with four ultra-handy chapters: Keep Things Clean, Banish Clutter!, Care for Clothes and Kitchen Hacks. Like all the chapters in the book, these four feature "Gotta Have 'Em!" roundups of tools and supplies, "The Big Buy" GHI-reviews of appliances,

furniture, and more, plus ways to "Cash In!" on your no-longer-needed items and "Family Matters" advice on getting your crew involved. After that, the Decorate It Yourself and Take It Outside chapters cover the pretty stuff—indoors and out—with easy-to-follow steps on painting, gardening and everything in between. To finish, the chapters on Easy Entertaining and how to Fix Stuff & Save Money round out what's important: the ability to live well—and enjoy it with friends and family.

My parents will probably be amused by the first list above, knowing how few of those things I still do. (I even left *out* navigating a boat, jump-starting a car, knitting and sponge painting! It was the 1990s.) But the point is that anything is possible, particularly if you learn how to do it yourself. And the best part? It's easier than you think. Please use and enjoy this book with that in mind. It was made with care.

—Jane Francisco
Editor in Chief
Good Housekeeping

neat: a tiny bedside shelf!

BEDDED BLISS

Keep your bedroom clutter-free by stationing adequate storage for your needs. Consider displaying your books on a coffee table instead of piled on the nightstand. A tiny bedside shelf helps keep necessities handy and within reach.

chapter

1

GOOD HOUSEKEEPING

KEEP THINGS CLEAN

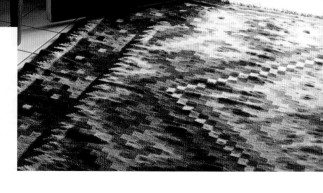

STOP DIRT IN ITS TRACKS

Clean floors without lifting a finger by doubling up on doormats: one outside each entryway and another inside—to catch twice as much schmutz. Also try a shoes-off-in-the-house rule. It's proven to keep floors cleaner longer.

CLEAR BRILLIANCE

The GH Institute–tested trick for spotless windows? Dust frames and sills first, then wash glass from side to side on one side and top to bottom on the other. If there are streaks, you can tell which side to re-do.

THROW IN THE TOWEL

They may not look dirty, but dish towels were deemed the most contaminated spot in the kitchen in a USDA-funded study. Change them out every couple of days, or even every day if you have a large family.

CLEAN SMARTER, NOT HARDER

Because how much do you *really* like doing it?

BE A TWO-TIMER

Forget trying to multitask. Better to use your time doing mini tasks during otherwise wasted minutes. Straighten a coat closet when your TV show goes to commercial, fold some laundry while on hold listening to call-center Muzak or unload the dishwasher as you wait for that pasta water to boil.

BUT STAY SINGLE-MINDED...

...when you're cleaning several rooms. Rather than tackling an entire room top to bottom, do one task from room to room. For instance, use a multipurpose spray on glass, metal and laminated or painted surfaces, then go back and polish wood furniture. You'll switch cloths and product containers less frequently—and finish faster.

USE LESS PRODUCT, NOT MORE

While it's tempting to spray down a window or mirror with glass cleaner, or spritz wood polish directly on furniture, don't. Instead, squirt solution on your cloth or sponge. This saves you product *and* effort—less wiping and, in the case of wood furniture, less dusting, since most polishes can leave a filmy buildup that attracts the pesky particles.

THAT'S GENIUS! Upcycle a **plastic or metal clothes hanger** to hold your paper towel roll as you clean room to room—first snip the hanger's crossbar in the center. Hang it on a knob to free up your hands and make it easier to pull off sheets.

TAKE COVER

No one is suggesting you cover your
furniture with plastic like the parents in
My Big Fat Greek Wedding (nor should
you use Windex® to fix every ailment!).
But when it comes to taking care of your
stuff—and cleaning less—prevention is
key. Invest in some stylish slipcovers
for upholstered pieces. White matches
everything and is simple to bleach.

GOTTA HAVE 'EM!
CLEANING ESSENTIALS

Look no further: The Good Housekeeping Institute recommends
all of these hard-working supplies.

MULTI-SURFACE SPRAY

Want squeaky-clean mirrors, countertops, painted walls and more? Meet your new best friend—a do-it-all solution like SPIC'N SPAN® CINCH® GLASS.

PAPER TOWELS

In addition to soaking up spills, these disposable sheets do double-duty: Use them to line drawers in the fridge or layer them between stacked pots and pans.

FURNITURE POLISH

A good wood polish—and GUARDSMAN® is one of the best—clears away dust *sans* streaks and leaves furniture residue-free. Use it to extend the life of your wood pieces.

MICROFIBER CLOTHS

Made from super-fine fibers, these reusable squares really pick up and trap dirt. Meaning? They can be used with just plain water, depending on the task.

BATHROOM AND KITCHEN CLEANER

No need to bust out the bleach with CLR® BATH & KITCHEN CLEANER: It cuts through soap scum, mineral stains and grease while shining chrome and whitening grout.

ELECTROSTATIC SWEEPER

SWIFFER®'s dry sweeper forever changed the way we clean floors by reaching places— and nabbing fine debris— that most vacs and brooms can't. Use the disposable cloths or Swiffer dusters to clean TV and computer screens and other delicate surfaces, too.

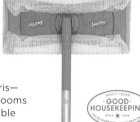

QUALITY TESTED
·GOOD·
HOUSEKEEPING
Since 1909
LIMITED WARRANTY - please see for details

FRESHEN FAST!

Grab these everyday items to zap odors on the double.

MAKE LEMON AID

Lemons smell clean, so try this: Cut one in half, put the pieces in a microwave-safe bowl with water to cover and heat on High for two to three minutes. While you enjoy the citrus scent, the steam softens hardened splatters inside the oven. Then, grind the fruit in the garbage disposal to eliminate any mustiness and greasy gunk.

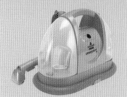

TO STEAM-CLEAN CARPETS

When your wall-to-wall carpet takes a beating, you may consider renting a carpet extraction cleaner (aka, a steam cleaner) to DIY. But cleaning thoroughly without damaging the fibers or oversaturating the carpet pad can require patience. No time (or desire)? Call in the aces at **Stanley Steemer®** or **Sears® Carpet & Upholstery Care**, two services that scored best in GH Institute testing. (For local options, search angieslist.com for cleaners with good reviews.) Estimates for one room start at less than $100.

Just need to spot-clean your upholstery or area rugs? Consider **Bissell®**'s **Little Green Portable Carpet Cleaner ($100)**, which has the Green Good Housekeeping Seal, thanks to its energy- and water-efficient manufacturing and recycled plastic parts.

USE THE NEWS

When it comes to newspapers, both the paper and the ink absorb odors. So crumple some up and stuff it into stinky shoes, a smelly lunch bag, the bottom of your garbage can or even plastic food containers for a few days (make sure to wash and rinse the containers afterward). You'll breathe easier soon.

KNOW YOUR JOE

It's no wonder perfume departments often display little bowls of coffee beans or fresh grinds—one big sniff quickly rids your nostrils of lingering aromas. Employ the same tactic in your fridge or freezer, the mudroom, on a shelf in your teenager's closet or anyplace that gets overly ripe.

GOOD PETKEEPING

Fur everywhere? Odor overwhelming? Puddles multiplying?
Try these tricks to minimize Mr. Whiskers's mess.

DE-STINK your dog between baths:
Lightly sprinkle her fur with baking soda,
rub it in and then brush it out.

DE-FUZZ upholstery, drapes and even
clothes with the easy-to-grip Scotch-
Brite® Upholstery Pet Hair Remover. Or
go low-tech and dampen clean rubber
gloves to collect the fur.

UNDO STAINS (of the bodily fluid kind)
with Bissell's pet stain removers, which
have the GH Seal. No time to shop? Try
the DIY method on page 139.

PREVENT SPILLS with an inexpensive
rubber pet placemat that stops bowls
from sliding and protects floors from
food and water splatters.

SPEED CLEANING

Go on, be lazy, er, strategic! You'll save time by putting off these tasks.

CLEANING OUT THE FRIDGE

Why bother doing it before trash day? Or, if you miss the garbage truck, wait to toss spoiled or expired food until the day you go grocery shopping. That way, you'll make room for incoming food, have a better idea of what items you need to restock *and* avoid having stinky leftovers hanging out in your trash bin for too long.

DUSTING THE BATHROOM

The time to do it: when you're changing out your used hand towel or towels. Then, you can use the terry cloth, preferably damp, to wipe down those dusty surfaces (e.g., counter and toilet tops—and anything on top of them; baseboards). This quick once-over will cut down on your need to deep clean more frequently.

GOOD HOUSEKEEPING — QUALITY TESTED — Since 1909 — LIMITED WARRANTY - please visit for details

SEAL ALL-STAR
MR. CLEAN® MAGIC ERASER®

Launched in 2003, this little white pad is the gold standard for nixing tough stains from hard surfaces—no harsh chemicals required. But how does it work? The Magic Eraser is made from melamine resin foam, the material used in insulation. Water activates "microscrubbers" that remove and trap dirt—and that, as the MTV crowd says, is where the magic happens.

WASHING DISHES BEFORE YOU PUT THEM IN THE MACHINE

Yes, you should scrape any food scraps into the garbage, but don't bother handwashing or even rinsing your dishes before you put them in the dishwasher. Research shows that it doesn't get your dishes any cleaner—and our GH Institute experts agree—as long as you don't let dishes sit before washing.

FAMILY MATTERS

How to split up chores evenly? Set aside an hour or two each week for cleaning. Write tasks on slips of paper and put them in bowls according to difficulty. Have each family member choose from the appropriate bowl—then have the crew get to work!

16 MINUTES TO A CLEAN HOUSE

Your place is a mess, and guests are on their way. Don't. Freak. Out. Just use this 4-step plan to have a presentable pad in minutes.

1 START WITH THE BATHROOM. Use an all-purpose cleaning wipe to clean the sink, countertops and toilet top. Clean the mirror and fixtures, straighten the shower curtain and hang fresh towels. *Time: 4 minutes.*

2 MOVE ON TO THE KITCHEN. Hide dirty dishes and cookware in the dishwasher if empty; if not, hide them in the oven. Use a wipe to clean the counters. *Time: 2½ minutes.*

3 DECLUTTER AND DUST THE LIVING SPACES. Put newspapers, magazines, shoes and other clutter into a shopping bag or laundry basket, then hide the bag or basket in a bedroom or closet—preferably one you use often, so it isn't forgotten. *Time: 4½ minutes.*

4 END WITH THE FLOORS. Vacuum main traffic areas and living spaces, including carpets and bare floors, with a rechargeable stick vac (see page 21 for a GH Institute–tested model). Store the vac, and greet your company! *Time: 5 minutes.*

IF YOU RUN OUT OF...

WINDOW CLEANER
Swap in 2 Tbsp. non-sudsy ammonia mixed with 1 quart (4 cups) water in a spray bottle.

LAUNDRY STAIN REMOVER
Swap in liquid dish soap or a few drops of hydrogen peroxide, which works like color-safe bleach.

SHOWER CLEANER
Swap in baking soda sprinkled on a damp sponge or a scrub brush.

GENTLE FABRIC DETERGENT
Swap in mild shampoo (and hand-wash in cool water in the sink).

TOILET BOWL CLEANER
Swap in 1 cup chlorine bleach. Pour into the bowl, swish clean with a brush, let sit 10 minutes and flush.

THE DON'T LIST

Before diving in, review these rules so you won't damage surfaces or fabrics.

1 DON'T USE VINEGAR ON STONE COUNTERS. It can etch and mar materials like granite. Use a mild stone cleaner, like Granite Gold®, instead.

2 DON'T MIX BLEACH WITH AMMONIA. Nor with ammonia-containing products, such as some window cleaners. When combined, they produce gas that can constrict breathing.

3 DON'T TRY BLEACH TO REMOVE RUST. It'll actually set the stain. Use a specially formulated rust-stain remover, such as GH-tested Whink®.

4 DON'T WASH YOUR CAR WITH DISH SOAP. It's harsher on the car's paint than a car wash. GH Institute pick: Simple Green® Car Wash, which also has the GH Seal.

5 DON'T CLEAN STONE FLOORS WITH VINEGAR. Just like countertops, the natural stone in your bathroom doesn't take kindly to acidic cleaners, like vinegar and lemon. Avoid ammonia, too, and stick to cleaning with special stone soap, or dish detergent and water.

6 DON'T USE LAUNDRY STAIN REMOVER ON CARPETS. It can leave a sticky residue that's a magnet for dirt. Go with a spray formulated for carpets (and check out the handy Bissell device on page 11).

7 DON'T DOUSE YOUR CARPET TO REMOVE A FRESH STAIN. Oversaturating the stain with water can damage the fibers, and excess moisture can leak through to the rug pad and flooring, where it can get trapped. Instead, employ the blot method for lifting stains. Lightly spritz with water to rinse (followed by more blotting with a clean, dry paper towel or cloth).

THE BIG BUY
VACUUM

Suck it up! A good vac is worth every penny when it comes to having the machine you need.

UPRIGHT

Best for: wall-to-wall carpeting and large rugs, as it loosens and removes embedded dirt better than other types of vacs. Evolved from the clunkers of old, most of today's uprights have hoses and attachments to mimic the versatility of canister vacuums. Take the sleek **ELECTROLUX PRECISION® BRUSHROLL CLEAN VACUUM CLEANER EL8805A**, which has a washable filter and easy-to-empty dust container. Its 3-in-1 attachment works on flat surfaces, in crevices and at a 90-degree angle—perfect for stairs and risers.

CANISTER

Best for: homes with many different surfaces and stairs. A straight-suction floor attachment (without a rotating brush) makes it great for cleaning hard-surface floors and low-loop carpets, while the hose reaches into tight spots and easily cleans upholstery and stairs. The low-noise **MIELE® 8990 COMPLETE C3 BRILLIANT** aced GH Institute tests to earn our GH Seal. Though this model is on the pricier side, good canisters by Hoover®, Kenmore®, Electrolux® and Panasonic® range from $150 to $750.

STICK VAC

Best for: quick pickups and light in-between cleanings. Much easier to store, not to mention carry, than traditional vacs, these slim suckers unfortunately don't offer the power or dust-cup capacity. But, man, rechargeable cordless sticks are convenient! The **HOOVER PLATINUM COLLECTION™ LINX CORDLESS STICK VACUUM BH500010** received an A in GH Institute tests for cleaning bare floors and eliminating pet hair on carpet.

WHAT'S THE DEAL WITH...

ROBOT VACUUMS?

These small, cordless machines use beam emitters or mapping technology to canvas your floors, sliding under beds and into corners, all while you're out running errands. The downside: Even top-testing models like the Neato Botvac 85 ($599) or Samsung®'s VR9000 ($999) can't deep-clean carpet.

CENTRAL VACUUM SYSTEMS?

Built into the walls of your home, with convenient inlets to plug in long-reach hoses, these systems may remove allergens better than traditional vacs. The downside: Some may need professional help to install.

HEPA FILTERS?

In vacuum cleaners, high-efficiency particulate air filters trap 99.97 percent of super-tiny particles, including dust mites, pollen and animal dander. The downside: None really—other than having to change the filters regularly.

PURGE THOSE PRODUCTS

Holding on to cleaners beyond their
recommended shelf lives can lessen
their efficiency. Write the date on the
label once you get it home from the store.
It's always best to discard any products
that have separated, clumped or gotten
lumpy, or have an off odor, no matter how
recently you've purchased them. Go to
cleaninginstitute.org for tips on disposal.

TAKE CARE OF YOUR TOOLS

Unless you clean your cleaning gear—and toss expired products—you could be pushing around grime and germs, or simply wasting your time. Here's how to handle it all.

BROOM

Vacuum the head with a handheld attachment or swish it in warm, soapy water; let dry, head down.

VACUUM

Empty the dirt receptacle after every couple of uses or replace the disposable bag before it's three-quarters full. Also change or wash the filters regularly.

MOP

Rinse or wash the strings, sponge or microfiber pad and squeeze out excess water. Hang the mop by its handle or stand it upside down to dry. Most strip and microfiber mop heads are removable and machine washable, too.

KITCHEN SPONGE

Once a week, soak the sponge for five minutes in a solution of 1½ Tbsp. chlorine bleach in 2 cups water. Launder any used cleaning rags weekly—or more frequently if needed.

On the wall (chalk writing):

TO DO :
buy juice
pick up cards
dry cleaning

WRITE ON YOUR WALLS

A bold chalkboard-painted accent wall in the kitchen is an eye-catching spot to jot down a daily to-do list or display a curated selection of your kids' art. Use adhesive-backed bulldog clips to hang their masterpieces.

2

GOOD
HOUSEKEEPING

BANISH CLUTTER!

vintage suitcases

SHOW SOME PERSONALITY

Organizing vessels don't have to be boring. Make the flea market or consignment shop your best friend, and find vintage suitcases, picnic baskets, trunks and more to hold items you want handy but tucked out of sight.

SOLVE THE LINEN CLOSET

Adopt these mess-taming tips: Store off-season bedding in bins. To retain their fluff, keep out pillows, comforters or any down-filled items, or only vacuum-seal them about 50 percent. Place dividers between towel piles and sheet sets, separated by bathroom or bedroom (master, guests, kids).

ANTI-WRINKLE ADVICE

The trick to repurposing gift bags? Keep them wrinkle-free. Rather than throwing them in a pile in your closet, use a file organizer to stand them upright. To revive wrinkled fabric ribbons: Iron them on low heat (you may need a spritz of water).

BE A WRAP STAR

If you give a lot of gifts throughout the year, do *yourself* a favor and create a station for wrapping presents. Musts: a tall vessel to hold rolls of specialty papers (no-tearing tip: Secure paper with loops cut from old tights) as well as rods to suspend rolls of frequently used wraps and ribbon.

ORGANIZING TRICKS THAT WORK

Try these simple solutions for real results. Your house will thank you.

WORK WITH YOUR HABITS

Does your husband dump out his pockets on the dresser every night? Don't fight it. Instead, set a decorative dish on top and a wastebasket below—and let him sort out what to keep and what to trash each evening. Similarly, if you like to try on or take off jewelry in the bathroom but then forget to put it away, place a small bowl on the counter to hold pieces. Once a receptacle is full, deal with its contents.

DEVELOP NEW ONES

The organizer's maxim: A place for everything and everything in its place. Assign spots for easily misplaced items, such as a hook by the back door for car keys, a tray on the coffee table for TV remotes or a holder for your reading glasses by the bed. Commit to returning things to their places, and you'll soon spend less time looking for stuff that's "lost."

STREAMLINE FURNITURE

With too many chairs or tables, even the most spacious room can look like an episode of *Hoarders*. To cut down on visual clutter and ease traffic flow, move out excess pieces. When investing in new furniture, focus on function *then* form. A coffee table or nightstand, for instance, should have at least one drawer, shelf or cabinet to keep items contained.

THAT'S GENIUS! The humble **shoebox** is often just the thing to hold, well, just about anything. Plus, it's free! Make sure to label what's inside, if you're putting the box away for storage. Or wrap the box and lid separately with decorative paper and leave it on display.

DECANT TO SAVE SPACE

Remove some TP, cotton balls and cotton swabs from the original packaging—and put them into reusable containers—to expand valuable inches in the bathroom vanity. Likewise, decant oversized bottles of mouthwash or pump (not aerosol) hair product into smaller vessels, so that they fit in the medicine cabinet or vanity, too.

PRACTICE SHELF PRESERVATION

Here's a novel idea: Cover the backs of bookcases with decorative paper, or paint the insides a poppy hue, and you'll be more inclined to show them off—and less likely to cover them up with clutter. Today's self-adhesive wallpaper makes it a snap to peel and stick.

RECLAIM THE JUNK DRAWER

It's time for it to hold its own! (You know, minus the clutter.)

1 Group the contents into categories (e.g., paper clips, rubber bands, coins, nails and screws), then relocate items that belong elsewhere, such as screwdrivers (toolbox) and bandages (medicine cabinet).

2 Eliminate duplicates or non-working items (locks without keys, broken toys). If you don't already have one, start a change jar so that you can cash in on its contents.

3 To finish, sort what's left into utensil dividers or small gift boxes. Order restored!

PREVENT PAPER CLUTTER

Cut those piles down to size with these smart tips.

MAKE AN ENTRANCE

The first step to eliminating paper clutter?
Bar it at the door. Subject every piece of
paper that comes into your house to the
"two Fs" test: If you can't file or frame it,
out it goes. Also try positioning two bins
in or near the foyer—one for recycling and
one for shredding—so that it's easier to
stay on top of those tasks.

CATALOG CHOICE

Visit catalog-choice.org to cancel unsolicited catalogs or download the free Catalog Spree (iOS) for digital versions of those you do want.

COZI

Want to streamline your family's schedules? Try Cozi, a free web service that helps you manage multiple calendars and lists as well as send messages and reminders directly to your family members' phones or email. Each person is assigned a color on the calendar, so you can easily reference who's going where and when.

TURBOSCAN

TurboScan Pro (iOS, $3.99) lets you scan and send a plethora of things: multipage documents, receipts for tax purposes, business cards for work. Meaning? You can toss the actual pieces of paper.

CLEAR THE DECK

Reclaim your out-of-control desktop: Take everything off its surface and replace the essentials. Then hang up daily-use references (e.g., a calendar) for speedy review. Organize what's left for storage: in drawers or cabinets or on shelves (if needed, corral items in dividers for faster scan-and-grab).

BEAT BUILDUP

Block off a half hour on your calendar once a month to clear out old catalogs, magazines and notes before they get out of hand. And if you're drowning in periodicals but don't want to give up your favorites, check out Texture. The tablet and smartphone app ($10 a month and up) allows you to read more than 150 different magazines (plus back issues) and individual articles.

THE BIG BUY
PAPER SHREDDER

Thwart would-be identity thieves by turning important docs into confetti. These two fared best in GH Institute tests.

FULL-SIZED

Best for: families who have a lot (but not a ton) to shred. With improved features that prevent paper jams caused by "overfeeding," a full-sized machine should provide solid service for years. The **FELLOWES POWERSHRED® 73CI** is a top choice for any home office prone to pop-ins from pets or kids, as it shuts off automatically if the paper slot is touched.

SPEED DEMON

Best for: those in a hurry with lots of paper to dispose of. The **ROYAL® CX80** rips through 28 feet of paper per minute (compared with the overall tested average of 16). A translucent bin lets you easily see when it needs emptying.

ALWAYS **SHRED** THESE

You may be tempted to shred everything—or nothing. To be safe, don't skip the following five types of documents.

• Anything you don't need that lists your Social Security number

• Unsolicited credit card offers

• Credit card statements and checks you no longer need

• Bank statements, brokerage, and mutual fund statements you no longer need

• Insurance claim offers you no longer need

BEFORE YOU BUY

Check the shred capacity before buying—it tells you how much your machine can handle before jamming. We recommend a sheet or two less than that.

BEFORE YOU SHRED

Line your bin with a shredder bag to make trash disposal quick and easy.

LOOK UP!

Use your walls, doors and other vertical surfaces to eke out as much storage space as possible.

GO ALL THE WAY

No one says you have to end your shelving before it reaches the ceiling, if that's what you desire—or that's how much stuff you need to stock. (Perk: It can make your ceilings look taller.) Buy or build add-on shelves for existing bookcases, and make sure to mount the unit to the wall.

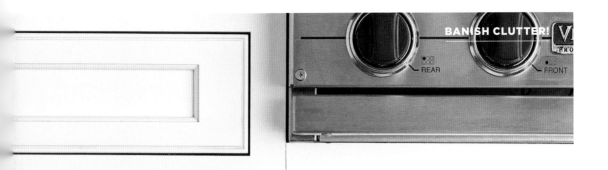

OPEN POSSIBILITIES

Kitchen drawer jammed with menus?
Bathroom counter a tangle of hair tools?
Disposable shopping bags stashed around
the house? Check *inside* your cabinets—
there's usually space to mount or hang
specialty holders on the door, such as
see-through pocket folders, a rack for
saucepan lids or a plastic bag dispenser
for under the kitchen sink.

BE A-DOOR-ABLE

Hanging shoe organizers are meant for shoes—but don't let that stop you! Inside a closet in your kid's room, they hold toys and other miscellany. Within an entryway closet, their pockets are perfect receptacles for small umbrellas, travel tissue packs, extra packs of chewing gum or other things you need when you're running out the door.

GOTTA HAVE 'EM! STORAGE STANDOUTS

These organizing finds are clever and chic. Just like you.

STYLISH BASKETS

Roomy baskets can jazz up your décor while helping you manage messiness. If you're looking to store holders on shelves, square or rectangular shapes fit better than round ones.

WALL HOOKS

Hooks 101: Make sure you have enough to do the job, whether it's to hang ties in the bedroom or towels in the bath. If you have too few (or ones that aren't sturdy enough), they'll be overrun and, ultimately, underused.

WHEELED BOXES

These plastic wonders will let you take back the space under your beds currently inhabited by dust bunnies.

HANDLED TRAYS

A smart way to corral items in clutter-prone zones (the kitchen counter, a foyer table): sleek trays that can be picked up— to relocate or repurpose—in a pinch.

LAZY SUSANS

Spinning organizers make the most of cramped cabinets. Look for split-level versions that let you stash twice the stuff!

MULTIFUNCTION FURNITURE

The beauty of lidded ottomans? Cheery stools like this one hold their contents *plus* whatever you place on top, be it a tray for drinks or your backside.

MAKE OVER
THE MUDROOM

Put clutter in its place (read: leave it in the entryway)
with these genius ideas.

SEAT YOURSELF

Discourage disorganization with a pretty
pillow-topped bench—it's the ideal place
to sit and remove muddy boots or rip open
mail. Non-lidded bins and baskets make it
easy to toss in or pull out (non-wet) shoes,
scarves, pet gear and more.

DOUBLE HOOKS

Choose coat hooks that have both top and bottom sections for extra spots to hang gear. Have young kids? Paint each a different color so they know which is theirs. Wicker picnic and fishing baskets transform mudroom chaos into calm.

MAXIMIZE CLOTHES QUARTERS

Whether you have an entryway closet or freestanding cabinets, don't skimp on sturdy hangers—basic metal hangers will bend under the weight of heavier coats (see page 45 for a GH Institute-recommended pick). Informal jackets can hang on hooks or pegs.

TUCK IT IN

Create a mini mudroom under your stairs.
Narrow, wall-mounted shelves are a sleek
spot for holding shoes and bags. A perfectly
proportioned umbrella stand sits neatly
against the wall. (Tip: The best stands allow
for air circulation, such as wicker, mesh,
slatted or open-sided styles.)

HOOK, DON'T HEAP

Avoid doubling up items on hooks, pegs or knobs. Otherwise, damp jackets won't dry well and may become funky smelling. See page 41 for a stylish solution.

GET AROUND

Take your organizing attempts from eyesore to artful by arranging your storage solution—like these drum-shaped catchalls—into a geometric display. Sturdy hatboxes (minus the lids) will produce a similar effect.

GOOD·HOUSEKEEPING QUALITY TESTED · Since 1909 · LIMITED WARRANTY · ghseal.com for details

SEAL ALL-STAR
JOY'S HUGGABLE HANGERS

HSN®'s organizing maven Joy Mangano came out with these slim, flocked hangers—and GH Institute quickly fell in love with them. Why? They save space in crowded closets and prevent slinky, slip-prone items from falling to the floor (plus, they come in 21 stylish shades).

ORGANIZING RULES OF THUMB

Practice these three lessons, and you'll be an organizing expert in no time.

1 PUT ITEMS WITHIN REACH. Constantly pulling out a step stool or stooping over to retrieve things? Always have to reach around or rifle through stuff to find what you need? Consider this an intervention. The most accessible storage is located in the space between your shoulders and knees. So, place items you use most often in this region—and position the things you use all the time in the *front* of the drawer, cabinet or shelf.

2 GROUP LIKE WITH LIKE. Example: Put all of the cooking utensils in one pottery container adjacent to the stove. When it comes to finding a place for seasonal items—like lawn furniture, sports equipment or holiday decorations—store them in the same area (e.g., attic, basement, garage or garden shed). That way, since you're rotating stuff in and out, there will always be a bit of space (think snow skis replacing water skis).

TO ORGANIZE YOUR HOUSE

Calling in an expert to help organize your home can pay off for years to come, particularly if you're time pressed or overwhelmed by decluttering to-dos.

Find a qualified pro on the National Association of Professional Organizers' site (**napo.net**). Hourly or project-based fees vary widely, though NAPO recommends *not* hiring based on price alone. "Focus on finding an organizer with a personality and skill set that matches your needs," it instructs. The downside to outsourcing? If you and your family can't or don't stick with the new system, it can be a waste of money.

If you simply need a fresh perspective on what to purge from a specific closet or room, invite over a decisive friend to provide moral support. Or check out sites like **clutterdiet.com.** It gives easy-to-follow programs for eliminating the junk (just like junk food) and measures your success in pounds.

3 LABEL IT— OR NOT.

If you're using see-through bins or canisters, labels are usually optional. The exceptions: if you have a lot of identical vessels (for, say, craft supplies or shoes) or if it might cue family members or guests where items go. For opaque holders (file folders, canvas boxes) or seldom-accessed seasonal or special occasion storage, labels save you search time. Trust us.

WEAVE AROUND

Stock the laundry room with easy-to-carry woven baskets—they're so much nicer to look at than plastic hampers. When not in use, tuck them onto open shelves. Pull them out to sort clothes.

GOOD HOUSEKEEPING

CARE FOR CLOTHES

DRESS FOR SUCCESS

Mount a hook outside your closet, or
hang one over the door, and each night
pull out an outfit to wear the next day.
Even if your closet stays impenetrable,
your a.m. routine will be simpler—and
you'll start the day in style.

sort by style
or color

KEEP VS. TOSS

Toss scented drawer liners and sachets,
whose oils can stain your lingerie. Instead,
tuck in an empty bottle of your favorite
perfume. Wrap it in a handkerchief to
ensure that it doesn't give off anything
but a hint of scent.

DIVIDE TO CONQUER

To instill some undergarment order, edit
out tattered, ill-fitting or uncomfortable
items (and be honest—you know you
hate wearing that scratchy lace bra).
Use inexpensive drawer dividers to give
everything a place.

LIGHTEN UP YOUR LAUNDRY LOAD

Doing the wash will always be a chore.
These expert tips make it feel a little less so.

DEAL WITH IT NOW

To make sure clothes aren't worse for the wear when they come *out* of the washer, first close zippers, hooks and snaps and tie straps and strings. Empty those pockets, too. Place a rail with clips or a small vessel nearby to hold anything you retrieve.

DEAL WITH IT LATER

When you spill coffee on your favorite blouse, there's no time to remove a fresh stain before work. So try a pre-treater that's safe to use up to several days before you wash, such as Shout® Advanced Ultra Gel Brush, which topped GH Institute tests.

AVOID THE HASSLE

Sort clothing *before* you reach the laundry room. There's no point in dragging it all there only to discover you don't have enough for, say, a full load of darks. And remember to keep items that shed (e.g., towels, sweaters, anything fleece or chenille) away from garments that attract lint, such as knits, synthetic fabrics and corduroy pants.

FAMILY MATTERS

Speed up the laundry-sorting process: Ask the family to pitch in. Opt for divided hampers for lights and darks, or go with separate baskets or bins for "delicates" and "everything else."

laun·dry
[lôn' drē, län'-] n., pl., -dries
1. dirty wash: dirty clothes or linen put aside to be washed
and ironed 2. clean wash: freshly washed clothes or linen
3. washing and ironing place: a place, especially a
commercial establishment or a communal room in a
building, where clothes and linen can be washed and
ironed [Early 16th century. Contraction of obsolete
lavendry < Old French lavenderie < Latin lavare "to wash"]

DOVETAIL YOUR TO-DOS

To save time and reduce fading, do
"machine-wash warm" and "cold" loads
together in cold water. Also, choose the
shortest wash cycle—after all, once your
clothes are clean, they're clean.

THE BIG BUY
WASHER

Find the right machine for your family's needs. These picks have been put through the GH Institute wringer!

FRONT-LOADER

Best for: saving energy *and* space—if your laundry area is cramped, you can stack this style. Front-loaders may cost more up front, but the machines use less water without sacrificing cleaning results, so you'll make your money back. The **ELECTROLUX 4.3 CU. FT. WASHER** speedily delivered very clean results. Its Fast Sanitize cycle makes short work of bacteria, and the Allergen cycle tackles dust mites and pet dander.

TRADITIONAL TOP-LOADER

Best for: tech minimalists. These straightforward machines still use agitators. Plus, some give you the freedom to add items after the cycle has started. There was much GH Institute liked about the affordable **KENMORE 3.6 CU. FT. TOP-LOAD WASHER WITH DEEP WASH CYCLE 22102**, including its energy efficiency, extra rinse feature and gentleness on clothes.

MODERN TOP-LOADER

Best for: washing clothes thoroughly yet gently, and being kind to your back. The newest top-loaders have pretty amazing perks. Take the **LG ULTRA LARGE CAPACITY FRONT CONTROL WASHER**— the buttons are front and center and a smaller, folding lid makes it less of a stretch to shut.

WASH YOUR
WASHER?

Yep, once a month for best results. Here's how.

• Select the largest load size, fill the tub with hot water and a cup of bleach, and run a cycle (on newer machines, just select the self-cleaning cycle).

• Alternatively, try a packaged washing machine cleaner, like GH Seal holder Tide® Washing Machine Cleaner, and use according to label directions.

• Remove dispensers and drawers and rinse them under hot water, brushing off residue.

• GH Institute tip: Leave the door of your front-loader cracked open between uses to let moisture escape (read: prevent mildew).

SIMPLE HOUSEHOLD WISDOM **55**

ALL DRIED OUT

The nuts and bolts of getting the most out of your dryer.

LET THE MACHINE DO THE WORK

Use your dryer's automatic cycle. The sensors detect a load's moisture and stop the tumbling when contents are dry. No auto option? A half hour is usually plenty for a light load.

DON'T DOUBLE UP ON DRYING

If you mix towels or sweatshirts with lightweight garments, the latter will get overly dried while the heavier ones play catch-up. Drying two separate loads saves time overall.

flat shelves for drying!

HOW TO IRON LESS

Take garments out of the dryer before they're completely dry. Give them a good shake, and hang clothes on round shouldered hangers—unless they're better off folded (see page 67 for details). If that's the case, lay them flat to dry.

USE YOUR KNIT WITS

To avoid extra wrinkles, make sure the dryer isn't overloaded—cramming creates creases. Also, choose a slower spin speed on the washer (so wrinkles on clothes aren't set in) and a lower dryer temperature. Remove knits promptly when the dryer stops.

GET THE WRINKLES OUT

Called a "godsend" by the GH Institute, this miraculous spray owes its smoothing power formula to a formula that coats and relaxes fibers. Just spritz and tug, and ripples disappear as fabric dries—in about five to ten minutes. The Downy® Wrinkle Releaser Plus is most effective on lightweight and medium-weight fabrics. For deeply wrinkled or heavier fabrics such as denim, use it in addition to ironing. Because it's water-based, it's not recommended for dry-clean-only materials, alas.

SET YOUR LINENS FREE

This may sound like extra work, but when drying large items like sheets and comforters, you'll want to frequently stop and readjust the load. Otherwise, the linens dry unevenly or may become balled up. (Dryers with drums that reverse-tumble throughout the cycle readjust automatically.)

GOTTA HAVE 'EM! WASHDAY WONDERS

Don't waste another minute on ineffective products.
These are the real deal.

SINGLE-USE DETERGENT PACKETS

Premeasured tabs save you the step of measuring liquid detergents. **TIDE PODS ORIGINAL** work well in both warm and cold water. Just be safe and keep these fun-looking packets away from curious kids and pets.

DETERGENT BOOSTER

Stop searching for stains, and simply toss one of these nifty packs—essentially a pouch of all-fabric bleach—in the washer. **OXICLEAN™ 2IN1 STAIN FIGHTER POWER PAKS** are a GH Institute favorite.

STAIN REMOVER

Uh-oh! Had a spot go through the dryer, and now it's seriously set? Squirt on a solution like **SHOUT ADVANCED GEL** and follow the package directions.

FABRIC SOFTENER

Whether you prefer a liquid formula, dryer sheets or spray-on softener like **METHOD®**'s, use it sparingly and avoid using it on towels, microfibers, sportswear and flame-retardant clothing. It can lessen the absorbency, wicking ability or other special properties of these fabrics.

SEPARATED SACK

Meet the **MUST-BE-NEAT LAUNDRY SORTER**. Place the compartmentalized holder inside a laundry basket to divide clothing items into three sections (think towels, socks and T-shirts). Pull the drawstring shut so that nothing falls out as you make your way through doorways and up the stairs.

EXTRA STORAGE

Keep detergents close at hand with a clip-on laundry shelf. Look for a 10-inch-deep style on organize.com to hold up to five 16-oz. boxes.

DEAL WITH DELICATES

Give your lingerie and "fancy" clothes the care they deserve.
Slash dry-cleaning costs while you're at it!

PROTECT YOUR UNDIES & BRAS

Really want to extend the life of your bras
and underwear? Zip them up in a mesh
delicates bag before machine washing
in cold water; also select the most gentle
cycle. This will keep the elastic in better
shape longer.

HANG THEM UP

Avoid putting bras in the
dryer—heat can wreak havoc on
their fibers. Smooth out lumps
or dents in padded cups. Then,
drape bras over coat hangers
(or lay flat) to dry.

PRESS DELICATES WITH A CLOTH

Good to know: If you top your lacy or
embellished blouse with a handkerchief or
clean dish towel and set the iron's temp to
match the fabric's most fragile fiber (e.g.,
nylon, silk), there's no need to go around
the delicate or decorated areas.

PROCEED WITH CAUTION

Did you know that manufacturers are required to list only one safe cleaning method on the label? So while dry-cleaning may give the best results, it may not be your only option. Still, hand-wash at your own risk: Fabrics or linings may shrink, and colors and trims can bleed.

And never wet-wash anything if the label says "dry-clean only" (look for "dry-clean" instead). Use cold water and spot-test before dipping. Once items are washed and rinsed, gently squeeze out water; reshape and lay flat to dry.

TRY A DRY-CLEANING SOLVENT

Have a stain on your favorite blazer? Spot treat it with a special cleaning fluid—Guardsman®'s is a GH Institute go-to. To minimize splotches, anytime, anywhere, pick up a stain pen, like Dryel® On the Go, that's safe for washable and dry-cleanable fabrics.

INVEST IN A GARMENT STEAMER

If your main reason for taking an item to the cleaners is to get it pressed, we don't blame you! But if the cost is a concern, invest in a garment steamer. Hold the garment taut and go over it lightly, allowing the steam to penetrate the fabric.

GET KITTED OUT

Sewing box essentials: buttons, needles in different sizes, sharp scissors, spools of thread in a variety of colors (cotton-covered polyester and 100-percent polyester are all-purpose types), straight and safety pins, a tape measure and a thimble.

ON THE MEND

Do damage control: These simple DIY solutions will give your tattered clothes new life.

PILLING Grab an emery board or a dry scrubber sponge, and lightly rub over the pills to remove them. This is safer on fabrics than "snipping off" pills.

SWEATER PULLS Turn the sweater inside out and, using a crochet hook or blunt needle, carefully pull the snag through to the backside of the fabric. Gently tug or smooth both sides of the yarn loop.

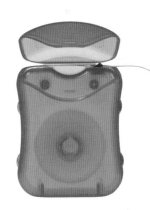

FALLEN HEMS Skip sewing and use fusible web tape. Cut a piece to the length of the fallen hem. Sandwich it between the fabric layers and press the fabric with an iron and set it to the appropriate temperature. Truly desperate? Try duct tape to secure a hem in a pinch.

LOOSE OR LOST BUTTON You're better off watching YouTube™ for a how-to-sew-on-a-button video. But here's a GH Institute–approved tip: Use monofilament fishing line to secure a button on heavy coat and jacket materials (velvet, wool, denim) *or* try unwaxed unflavored dental floss.

END CLOSET CHAOS

Because you shouldn't dread opening that door or drawer.

FIRST THINGS FIRST

The best way to conquer clothes clutter: Hold your own once-a-year fashion show. Empty the closet, and try on each garment in front of a full-length mirror. Does it fit? With what outfits and on what occasions will you wear it? Does it need mending? Separate pieces into four piles: keep, mend, donate, throw away. Follow the same steps for shoes. Now you can start organizing the keepers.

DITCH THE DOOR

Once your closet is organized, if it's still cramped inside, consider taking off the doors and hanging curtains instead. Not only will it give bulkier items a little more room to breathe, it can save you square footage, if the doors aren't pocket style. Bonus: Curtains give your bedroom a soft, relaxed look.

TO HANG OR TO FOLD?

The way you hang your clothes can make a big difference in a) whether you have to dewrinkle them and b) how long they'll stay in good condition. For instance, fold trousers along the crease and double them over the hanger bar, and hang skirts by their loops to avoid unwanted fold marks and stretching. When it comes to stretchy materials like knit or beaded garments, however, avoid hanging them at all— gravity is not your friend; the clothes will lose their shape. Instead, roll thin knits, just as you would when packing for a trip, and fold heavy or bulky ones. Fold and store beaded items flat.

DOES IT PAY TO HIRE A PRO?

TO INSTALL CUSTOM CLOSETS

If you've got the extra cash, by all means, have the Container Store® install its sleek **Elfa®** system (for an additional 30 percent of your total purchase), or call in a company like **California Closets®** to alleviate your storage concerns. The results—being able to quickly locate both of your black pumps on a harried morning—may be priceless.

If your budget is more modest, take heart: The DIY systems on the market start around $300 and can be installed by mere mortals. Ones by **ClosetMaid®**— particularly the Selectives® and ShelfTrack® lines— have done well in GH Institute observations of consumers assembling the systems. Just know, there may be some trial and error, and you should probably pick up a nice bottle of wine to celebrate with when you're all done. And partner up! Most systems require four hands!

DOUBLE YOUR (HANGING) PLEASURE

Many homebuilders default to "1R1S" or "one rod, one shelf" in closets, while most people (in this century at least!) don't have a wardrobe of only long dresses and coats. If you wear more separates, try installing a second clothing rod to maximize your hanging space. For a quick fix, buy a rod that hangs off the top one. You can set the width and height for a custom fit.

TURN OLD CLOTHES INTO $$$

If you're so over those once-coveted Stuart Weitzman® boots (hey, fashion is fickle), it may be time to shop your closet.

POSHMARK®, a free mobile app, lets stylish types see and buy your treasures on the fly. Create listings by snapping pics with your smartphone of items you want to sell. Poshmark takes 20 percent off your price, and the buyer pays for shipping.

TRADESY®, a digital buy-and-sell marketplace, features both high-end (Alexander Wang®, Gucci®) and brand-name (J. Crew®, Zara®) labels. Designer duds usually go for 65 percent off retail; other clothes, 70 to 75 percent off. The site takes just 9 percent.

PLATO'S CLOSET® is a hip resale shop (with about 400 locations across the United States) that buys teens' and 20-somethings' clothes—typically stuff that's been in stores within the past 12 to 18 months.

THREDUP®, an online consignment shop, sends you a Clean Out Bag to fill with clothes and ship back, postage paid. Within a month, they'll let you know what they'll buy and for how much; you earn up to 80 percent of the selling price (they accept kids' clothes, too).

TOP-DOLLAR TRICK

When you post, include several photos showing front, back and side views—even of the interior of a handbag and the soles of shoes. Note anything unique, such as a blazer's silk lining.

Donations

SWAP SMART

When it comes to storing your seasonal
clothes, don't save what you won't use.
If you find that there are pieces that you
haven't worn all winter or summer, donate
them to charity. Chances are you won't
wear them next year either.

DITCH THE MOTHBALLS

The traditional method of mothproofing winter wear in storage is on the outs. Experts say mothballs, which contain pesticides, can irritate eyes and skin and even affect the nervous system and liver. Try these safer ways to protect your cardigans.

CLEAN FIRST. Food and sweat stains are magnets for moths. Launder washables or dry-clean clothes before storing. Make sure laundered items are fully dry.

DON'T RELY ONLY ON CEDAR. The wood's oils may zap small larvae, but not large larvae or adult moths. Cedar lost its scent? Sand the wood to get it back.

SEAL IN AIRTIGHT CONTAINERS. This keeps out moths *and* moisture, which can lead to mold. Try vacuum-sealed bags.

DEAL WITH MOTHS. If you find them, move everything out and vacuum the carpet, walls and baseboards well (and toss the vacuum bag and dirt afterward). Scrub shelves and walls, then clean and store clothes properly.

BAG BASICS

Corral purses, wraps, etc., in a hanging bin with upward-slanting compartments so that items stay put, or along a shelf with dividers to stop totes from toppling over. Tuck in handbag handles to prevent damage. Hook belts and thin scarves onto separated hangers, or roll them and stow in a drawer or a bin.

DON'T FORGET THE ACCESSORIES!

They can really make an outfit. Here's how to wrangle bags, shoes, jewelry and more.

GO HEEL TO TOE. Arrange shoes front to back. It gives you a speedy survey of color, toe style and heel height to help speed up getting dressed.

FILE THEM IN A CONVERTIBLE SHOE RACK like Lynk®'s 15-pair style, which can be built vertically or horizontally to best suit your space.

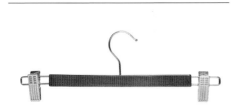

CLIP THEM UP. Even if you already have an over-the-door shoe organizer, it isn't always ideal for tall boots. Instead, attach boots to skirt hangers. (Clip over fabric to avoid marks on leather.) GH Institute tip: Keep the soles of hanging boots away from other hanging clothes.

OPT FOR SEE-THROUGH BOXES. Your pieces will stay dust- and damage-free.

1 SHOW IT ALL OFF. Turn your jewelry into decor: Drape it from a tree, pin it to a corkboard or let it shine through a glass vase or footed jar.

2 PREVENT TARNISH. Airborne chemicals and humidity are culprits. If you live on a busy street or near the ocean, store pieces in tarnish-resistant cloth bags.

3 KEEP IT NEAT. Use an ice cube tray to store earrings or a cutlery divider to separate necklaces and brooches.

DEVELOP SOME HANG-UPS

Jewelry becomes wall art when you string it up. Use hooks, knobs or even pushpins to suspend your favorite necklaces within easy reach. No more tangled chains! Here, L-hooks topped with wooden beads that are painted with nail polish transform a piece of wood into a necklace and bracelet tree.

BRING BACK THE BLING

Gold-and-gem rings all gunked up? Lotion, soaps and everyday dirt can clog the prongs, making stones appear facetless and flat. Give them a bath: Pour a few drops of mild dish soap into a small bowl of sodium-free seltzer water or club soda. Put the jewelry into a small strainer, and place it in the bowl to soak for about five minutes. Swish it around, fishing out each piece to go over settings and crevices with a soft toothbrush. Return items to the strainer and rinse under running water; dry with a soft cloth.

THAT'S GENIUS! Stack bangle bracelets on a **paper towel stand** so that you can see your favorites at a glance.

LIVE ON THE EDGE

While it may seem contradictory, sharp knives are actually safer to use than dull blades because they require less pressure to cut and don't slip as easily. For goof-proof sharpening, try GH Institute–tested Chef's Choice® ProntoPro Diamond Hone Knife Sharpener.

chapter

4

GOOD HOUSEKEEPING

KITCHEN HACKS

GO ABOVE AND BEYOND

Whether the issue is a lack of counter surfaces or no upper cabinets, installing a hanging rack above the work area is a sneaky way to maximize your storage space for frequently used tools and supplies.

hang a rack!

GROW YOUR OWN

Raise your hand if you've bought herbs for a meal only to have the rest of the bunch go bad before you could use it. If this happens more than you'd like to admit, conserve food (and money) by planting several of your family's go-to seasonings. Snip as needed.

GET SPICY

To get your spice collection in order, replace dried herbs and spices every two years (at least). Buy spices you don't use frequently in smaller jars. Flip to page 92 for more ideas.

MAKE IT CLEAR

See-through jars are a pantry no-brainer: Knowing what you have on hand and how much saves you a trip to the market.

EXPAND YOUR WORKSPACE

For versatility, the only thing better than
a built-in island is a non-built-in one. Opt
for one with drawers to provide ample
storage for cutlery, pots and baking
supplies. Hang ladles or potholders from
the sidebars. If space allows, add counter-
height chairs so that family and friends
can keep you company as you cook.

DECLUTTER
THE KITCHEN

Stop fighting with the jumble of stuff in your cupboards and fridge—
and streamline your cooking routine. Save a little money, too!

END THE LID AVALANCHE. Genius idea: Use a low-profile dish drainer to line up pot lids in a drawer. Drawers not deep enough? Look into nifty cabinet door-mount organizers.

PULL OUT. Difficult to see what's in the back of your cupboards? Retrofit them with slide-out shelves to access their recesses easily.

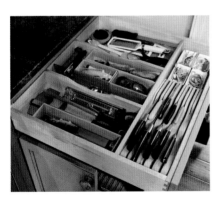

COMPARTMENTALIZE. Use slim trays and drawer dividers to neatly corral kitchen gadgets. An in-drawer knife block keeps blades sharp—and hidden from kids.

CLIP AND SAVE. Use clips to seal snacks, baking supplies or anything that could go stale quickly or attract pests. Clear dividers make items visible.

DE-STRESSED DINNER PREP

Make meal time easier—from the store to the kitchen.

MAKE A MASTER LIST

Keep track of pantry supplies by listing items on a chalk or dry-erase board in the kitchen. Mark an X next to a food when you use the last of it; use this to make your list on shopping day (wipe off the Xs to start again). Or do it digitally: Instacart.com, a grocery delivery service, has a list-making feature that you can use even if you don't order groceries from them.

COUPONS

Every day, hundreds of printable grocery coupons are available on coupons.com, or you can load them onto its mobile app, Coupons.

KEYRING

Capitalize on your frequent-shopper status: Use the free Key Ring app to snag discounts and freebies at Safeway®, CVS®, Target®, Ralphs®, Trader Joe's® and more.

IBOTTA® AND CHECKOUT 51

Don't bother Instagramming your food—shoot your receipts instead! Free apps like Ibotta and Checkout 51 give you cash back for select items, as long as you upload a photo of the receipt as proof.

PLAN FOR UNPACKING

When loading food into the shopping cart and again when bagging at checkout, group items according to where they're stored at home—in the fridge, freezer or pantry. Harmful bacteria multiply at room temperature, so the quicker you can chill perishables, the better.

COOK AHEAD

Handle particularly busy nights by precooking meals. For instance, if you know your daughter's Girl Scout meeting is every Tuesday, prepare two meals on Monday nights—and store the second in airtight containers in the fridge. Or designate one Sunday a month for advance cooking.

kitchen multitasker!

MAKE FRIENDS WITH THE MICROWAVE

Sure, you use it to pop popcorn and heat leftovers, but it can do *so* much more. The basics: defrosting meat, melting chocolate, softening butter and softening lemons and limes for easy juicing. More advanced: making perfect polenta, "roasting" spaghetti squash, "baking" potatoes and "poaching" delicate fish (cook it right on the platter!).

CUT CORNERS, NOT FLAVOR

Speed up the dinner dash by getting the most out of these gadgets and gear.

PASTA POT WITH COLANDER INSERT
This duo is perfect for cooking pasta or vegetables *without* having to carry the pot to the sink to drain. Just lift the strainer, give it a couple of shakes over the pot and you're ready to serve.

MINI CHOPPER No need to haul out the cutting board and knife to chop a single onion or carrot, or a handful of herbs. Opt for a mini that has a dishwasher-safe bowl.

PRESSURE COOKER The fast cousin of the slow cooker, this sealed pot makes meals imminently faster than other methods (e.g., one hour for meat-falling-off-the-bone ribs). Pick one with a thick aluminum bottom to prevent food from burning.

GRILL PAN When the weather isn't ideal for outdoor grilling—or your time is tight—an enameled grill pan will do the trick. Bonus: It's a cinch to clean and doesn't need to be seasoned after each use.

THE PERFECT PAN

Unlike your basic cookie sheet, which has only one or two curved sides for easier handling, a jellyroll pan has 1-inch-high sides. Perfect for making cake rolls, it can double as a cookie sheet or pizza stone and is terrific for roasting veggies, baking large batches of bar cookies or brownies and catching drips underneath bubbly casseroles and pies. You're welcome.

FAMILY MATTERS

An impressive 21 million children ages 17 and under watch the Food Network®. And Fox®'s *MasterChef Junior* and other shows now give them a TV avenue to show off their skills. Cooking together is a fun, affordable activity that can help kids gain key life skills. (Plus, not even a picky eater can resist tasting tilapia he herb-crusted himself!) Encourage your child to log favorite recipes in a spiral-bound "cookbook." She'll feel accomplished as she keeps track of her culinary creations.

GOTTA HAVE 'EM!
MEAL-PREP MUST-HAVES

The GH Institute Kitchen Appliances Lab and Test Kitchen teams can't live without these tools.

HAND BLENDER

Use this tool to puree or blend right in the pot, glass, bowl or even pan—eliminating any messy transfer to a countertop blender. Look for ones like the **CUISINART® SMARTSTICK® CSB-77** that come with attachments (e.g., whisk, chopping blade).

12-INCH TONGS

Tongs are ideal for flipping meat because you don't have to pierce it—and let out juices—to do so. Consider them a safe way to extend your reach—to shift hot things in the oven or even grab items on high shelves.

SALAD SPINNER

Who has the time to let washed veggies air-dry? Exactly. The **KITCHENAID® SALAD AND FRUIT SPINNER** has three removable dividers that allow you to spin-dry different foods at the same time without mixing them.

SIZEABLE SKILLET

One-pan meals are wonderful for two reasons: less prep *and* less cleanup. The **ANOLON® AUTHORITY 12.5" COVERED DEEP SKILLET** heats evenly on gas and electric ranges.

AIRTIGHT STORAGE

Glass food containers always keep air out better than plastic ones in GH Institute tests, particularly **SNAPWARE®'S TOTAL SOLUTION™** line. Bonus: You can safely use them in the freezer, oven (without the covers), microwave and dishwasher.

SILICONE SPATULA

Don't waste a drop with one of these flexible scrapers. It gets into the very corners of a pan and leaves nothing behind in bowls. Grab it when you're making soups, sauces or batter.

KEEP FOOD FRESH LONGER

Follow these simple steps to make sure your food is safe and cut down on waste.

GIVE IT AIR

Don't overstuff your refrigerator—air needs room to circulate so that the appliance can work efficiently. The opposite is true with storage vessels: Fill containers almost to capacity, and remove as much air as possible from zip-seal bags or when wrapping items—in the fridge, freezer or on pantry shelves.

Set your fridge to 37°F, and follow these storage tips for food safety.

DAIRY & EGGS

Eggs: 3 to 5 weeks

Milk: 1 week

Butter: 1 to 3 months

Yogurt: 1 to 2 weeks

MEAT

Deli-sliced lunch meat: 3 to 5 days

Raw chicken or turkey: 1 to 2 days

Leftover cooked meat: 3 to 4 days

Raw ground meat: 1 to 2 days

FRUITS & VEGETABLES

Apples: 4 to 6 weeks

Citrus: 1 to 3 weeks

Berries: 7 to 10 days

Grapes: 1 week

Peppers: 4 to 14 days

Mushrooms: 3 to 7 days

Lettuce: 1 to 2 weeks

Corn on the cob: 1 to 2 days

CONDIMENTS

Mayonnaise: 2 months

Bottled salad dressing: 1 to 3 months

Ketchup: 6 months

GO WITH THE GRAIN

Store grains and cereals in the fridge to preserve their freshness—particularly if you live in a warm climate. When it comes to bread, however, pop it in the freezer if you fear it may go stale or get moldy too soon (the fridge can dry it out). Toast or thaw as needed.

THE SPICE IS RIGHT

Shelf risers or a tiered rack let you see all of your spices at a glance—so you'll cook with them more often. (DIY idea: Stack empty aluminum foil or plastic wrap boxes under spice jars to get the same effect.) Whenever you buy a new seasoning, add a small sticker to the bottle and write the purchase date on it.

THE BIG BUY
REFRIGERATOR

Stay cool: Read these reviews before you invest in your next fridge.

FRENCH DOOR

Best for: flexibility—you can store wide platters yet also access one side of the fridge without letting warm air into the whole thing. As with side-by-side models, this style needs less clearance to open doors. Ones like the GH Institute–tested **WHIRLPOOL GOLD® FRENCH DOOR REFRIGERATOR** are great for families, because they boast spacious pizza-fitting freezers, a smudge-free finish and more.

SIDE-BY-SIDE

Best for: convenience—no pulling out freezer drawers; in-door icemakers and water dispensers come standard. The best models, like **FRIGIDAIRE®'S GALLERY 25.5 CU. FT. REFRIGERATOR**, have the largest-capacity crisper drawers, humidity-controlled crispers and digital settings.

FREEZER ON TOP

Best for: tight budgets. These are the least expensive since they're no frills. But other styles' perks like the built-in water dispenser/ice maker add to electricity costs—freezer-on-top configurations use 10 to 25 percent less power—and these features are the most likely to break. The **WHIRLPOOL®'S 28-INCHES WIDE TOP-FREEZER REFRIGERATOR WITH IMPROVED DESIGN** passes GH Institute inspection.

REPAIR OR
REPLACE?

How to know when you need a new appliance:

• **With any appliance,** GH Institute recommends replacing it if the repair cost is more than half the cost of a new one.

• **For the fridge,** if your machine is no longer keeping contents cold (below 40 degrees), or if it's more than 15 years old, consider replacing it. You may be paying $150 a year to run an old unit (especially if it predates 1997, when the Energy Star label became available).

• **GH Institute tip:** The US government has a $300 million fund for rebates on energy-efficient appliances. Go to your state's energy-office site for info (naseo.org/members-states)

CLEANING CHEATS

Minimize post-meal messiness in minutes.

STOVE-TOP TRICKS

Want to make stove-top cleaning easier? Cover adjoining burners with extra pot lids when sautéing. The lids are a much quicker cleanup than the burners. In the oven, if a spill happens, immediately and liberally sprinkle it with salt to soak up the liquid. When it cools, nudge the crusty stain loose with a spatula; wipe clean.

FULLY LOADED

The debate over the best way to load the dishwasher ends here.
Follow these GH Institute–tested tips.

UTENSILS GO UP AND DOWN Forks: prongs up. Spoons: some up, some down to avoid nesting, which makes them harder to clean. Knives: blades down for safety.

FACE DISHES INWARD Load with the dirty sides facing the center, where the spray is the strongest.

STOP SPOTS Nestle glasses between tines—if they go over them, drops may dry where tines touch glasses; also, glasses can shift around and crack.

COMMON MISTAKE! Placing platters along the front of the bottom rack can interfere with the detergent being fully dispensed.

HAND-WASHING HOW-TO

1 To remove hard water deposits on nice glassware: Warm 2 cups of white vinegar in the microwave for two minutes and pour it into a plastic basin.

2 Place glasses, on their sides, in the vinegar. Soak for three minutes. Rotate as needed, so all surfaces of the glass are bathed in vinegar.

3 Rinse them in clear water and dry with a lint-free towel.

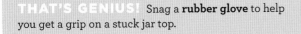

THAT'S GENIUS! Snag a **rubber glove** to help you get a grip on a stuck jar top.

THE PRETTY STUFF

You spend enough time in the kitchen; it ought to look nice.

CHIC AND CHEAP

Freestanding shelves are simpler (and less pricey) to put up than cabinets and give a breezy, casual feel to a kitchen. Open, slide-out shelves make cooking gear stashed in wicker easy to access.

SOOTHE THE PALETTE

An understated color scheme of soft grays and white turns your kitchen into a Zen retreat. Reflective finishes—polished marble floor, stainless steel appliances—make the room appear larger.

ADD A LITTLE POP

A cheery red banquette cushion invigorates the eating nook in the same kitchen. No built-in seating? Top chair seats with colorful cushions or drape the table with a bright cloth.

SEAL ALL-STAR
CAESARSTONE® QUARTZ COUNTERTOPS

Our GH Institute experts were so wowed by Caesarstone's quartz countertops that they installed them in all of our Labs and the Institute Test Kitchens. Caesarstone is scratch-, heat-, mildew- *and* stain-resistant, no sealant needed (granite, which is more porous, must be sealed periodically). Caesarstone countertops are made from resilient material (93% quartz, 7% polyester resin) that is ideal for kitchens and bathrooms. And its on-trend lines mean you don't have to sacrifice style for durability.

FOCUS ON CLEAN DESIGN

In a clutter-free kitchen, high-end touches—
like brass knobs, a small chandelier and
a marble mosaic backsplash—elevate
everything around them. The matte
black sink faucet seems sculptural when
contrasted with the pale surroundings.

**TO REFINISH
CABINETS**

If you're not
known for your
patience or
precision, a
professional cabinet
makeover may be
worth the splurge.
After all, you have
to remove the door
and drawer fronts,
be careful around
cabinet lips and
ledges and wait for
each coat of paint
or stain to dry.
Basically it's not a
simple weekend
afternoon project.

However, if
you've got a good
dose of DIY spirit
and a couple of
days to spare,
**Rust-Oleum®
Cabinet
Transformations®**
makes it easy to get
a custom look for
less. Promising no
stripping, sanding
or priming plus no
special skills
required, the kit
comes in two sizes,
depending on the
size of your
cabinetry (100 or
200 square feet),
and dozens of
fresh finishes.

SOFTEN UP

The quickest low-cost way to change
the look of your kitchen? Swap out
the dish towels. (Extra credit: Update
a cafe curtain over the sink.)

prints pop in white frames!

INSTANT WALL ART

Don't waste a scrap: Raid your sewing bin or hit the fabric store for coordinating samples. Showcase them in matching frames, hung in a grid for maximum impact.

chapter

5

GOOD HOUSEKEEPING

DECORATE IT YOURSELF

bamboo makes a perfect rod

HEADBOARD REFRESH

To make over a lackluster headboard, grab a graphic woven rug, a sturdy rod, some rope and your toolbox. Hold the rod against the wall; drill two screws into the wall near each end, leaving ½ inch of each screw exposed. Wrap rope around the rod; hang on the screws. Drape your rug over top. Va-va-voom!

ADD ARCHITECTURE

Living in a featureless box? Crown moulding along the ceiling or a chair rail around the center of the room lend character and style. Buy unfinished wood trim, cut it to fit your space, and then paint the pieces to match.

PEELING WALLPAPER

Put it back in its place with Red Devil's House & Home Restore™ Wallpaper Seam Repair. In GHI tests, it held up even in high humidity. Use the thin applicator to get behind raised seams; then press down gently for a minute and wipe off any excess.

HAVE HIGH IDEALS

Living in a place with low ceilings? Choose "short" furniture—pieces that are low and long (e.g., sofa, media cabinet, dresser). Together, they'll emphasize a horizontal line that's far from the ceiling, drawing the eye down so the space feels taller.

FOCUS ON THE FOYER

Painting this first-impression area a bold color gives you more bang for your buck. Why? Entryways tend to be smaller than, say, living rooms, so you won't need to cover so much square footage.

EASY ROOM MAKEOVERS

These speedy DIY solutions are totally worth the effort
(and won't break the bank!).

REARRANGE THE FURNITURE

If your space's style has gone stale, try
this free fix: Rearrange the furniture.
But *before* you lift the sofa, consult
a no-cost app like Home Design 3D
Free (iOS only) to create a three-
dimensional visualization. Then, go
on and move pieces around at will.

DO THIS BRICK TRICK

Transform a dated redbrick
fireplace with white or cream
paint. Small accents—such as two
turquoise vases on a coffee table
or mantel—really pop against a
pale backdrop.

ESTABLISH BORDER

Use an area rug to define a "room" in open space. And don't skimp on the carpet's size—one that's too small can shrink the zone. In the living room, make sure it's large enough so that the front legs of key furniture pieces are on it.

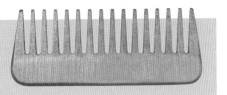

THAT'S GENIUS! Gently untangle fringe on carpets, upholstery and drapes as well as tasseled pulls with a **wide-toothed comb.**

STRIKE IT RICH

Metallic accessories lend polish to any
room while adding a warm, luxe touch.
But you don't need all the gold in Fort
Knox to copy the gilded look. A coat or
two of gold or brass spray paint quickly
updates decorative tables, light fixtures,
vases and more.

PRETTY UP PULLS

Update a drab dresser or any plain cabinet with a set of colored or decorative crystal knobs. The faceted pulls feel fancy (even if you opt for plastic versions). Think of them as jewelry for your furniture.

CHEER UP WITH POM-POMS

Pom-pom and tassel trims look *and* feel fun. Use one to embellish basic curtains or overhaul a pillow. For most projects, you don't even need a sewing machine—grab some fusible webbing and your iron, and you're set.

GROWN-UP PASTELS

Why relegate these soft shades to kids'
rooms? Sophisticated pastels—pale blue,
yellow or green; pink, peach or lavender—
lend serenity to your living spaces.
Colored pillows and lamp shades are an
affordable way to try a new scheme.

CAN'T-FAIL COLOR COMBOS

Designer trick: Look through your closet to determine which hues you prefer—and let them inspire your next decorating project. Here are a few that GH loves:

KELLY GREEN + GRAY Soft gray grounds feel-good green for a style that's at once earthy and energetic.

NAVY + TANGERINE Pops of tangy orange wake up classic navy. Layer in white for a casually crisp look.

TEAL + TAN Imagine sea glass nestled in beachy sand. This soothing palette is Mother Nature–made for decorating.

MAGENTA + RED Nothing packs a punch like vibrant hot pink. Well, nothing other than layering it with red.

PAINT A ROOM IN A DAY

Sample your shade (or several) in your space to see how it looks throughout the day. Then, follow these GH Institute–tested steps.

1 **COVER UP.** Use fabric drop cloths to protect the floor and any furniture from paint splatters and spills.

2 **CLEAN FIRST.** Paint won't adhere as well to a dirty surface, so first use a microfiber sweeper to remove dust, cobwebs and soot from the walls. Swab down extra-grimy parts with a wet sponge or cloth; let dry.

3 **PATROL THE BORDERS.** Remove outlet and light-switch covers, and tape off any areas you don't want painted.

4 **PICK YOUR PAINT.** Use one with a built-in primer, like Benjamin Moore® Aura® ($70 per gallon), to cover a dark wall with a light color in a fraction of the time (thanks to fewer coats). Going from light to light? Two coats of good-quality regular paint should do it.

5 **START IN THE CORNERS.** With an angled brush, paint a 2-inch border around taped-off areas as well as the ceiling. Then, fill in the central unpainted space using a paint tray and roller in overlapping W- or M-shaped strokes. Let the first coat dry for at least a couple of hours, then coat again. Have a moist rag handy to wipe fresh splatters.

6 **FINISH UP.** Rinse your paintbrush and roller under a faucet until the water runs clear. Decant the tray's leftover paint back into the can; seal the can tightly. Rinse your tray or throw away the liner.

7 **LEAVE NO TRACE.** Scrape off dried drips with a credit card or plastic spatula. Remove painter's tape before you call it a night, pulling it off at an angle to avoid tearing the finish.

QUALITY TESTED GOOD HOUSEKEEPING GREEN LIMITED WARRANTY. ghseal.com for details

SEAL ALL-STAR
WORTHY OF YOUR WALLS

Green Good Housekeeping Seal holder Benjamin Moore Natura® goes on smooth, and in just one coat, it covers as well as (if not better than) a coat of primer plus paint. In GHI tests, this zero VOC (volatile organic compound) was fade- and stain-resistant, making it an attractive option for many rooms in your home.

GOTTA HAVE 'EM!
PAINTING ESSENTIALS

Don't start your project without this gear.

PAINTER'S TAPE

Painter's tape protects moldings, baseboards and window frames, and comes off more easily than regular masking tape. Both the green and yellow (delicate) FrogTape® have the GH Seal.

ANGLED BRUSH

Pick up a 2-inch angled brush for the best control when edging around ceilings and taped areas.

PAINT TRAY AND PLASTIC LINERS

Do you *really* need liners? Only if you want to deal with a *lot* less mess! You can even ball up and throw out Peel-a-Tray liners when you're done.

FABRIC DROP CLOTH

Choose a canvas cover instead of plastic. The latter can be slick under your feet.

ROLLER FRAME AND EXTENSION POLE

The roller frame is what your cover slips onto. For easier detachment, try a quick-release frame-handle holder by Shur-Line®. Another worthy investment: a pro-style Purdy® extension pole.

ROLLER COVER

The wrong nap will apply too much or too little paint. Use this rule of thumb: Look for one with a $\frac{1}{4}$-inch nap for smooth surfaces, $\frac{3}{8}$-inch for semi-smooth or $\frac{5}{8}$-inch for rough or textured.

MAKE SMALL SPACES LIVE LARGER

Maximize your square footage—or at least its appearance—
without changing addresses.

ADD NATURAL ELEMENTS

Fresh bouquets and botanical prints as
well as wicker baskets and a sisal area
rug all blur the distinction between the
indoors and out. Use them throughout
small rooms—or your entire house—to
keep from feeling hemmed in.

TRICK OUT TIGHT CORNERS

Mount a clever corner ledge above a door to display candles or other decorative touches. Similarly, freestanding or built-in corner cabinets can make all the difference in storage-starved bathrooms, entryways and kitchens.

DIVVY IT UP

Open floor plans are more spacious, right? Not necessarily. A cavernous room can become a chaotic waste of space unless you establish inviting zones. Divide one into separate rooms with an open-back bookcase that's half-filled.

REFLECT ON THIS

A wall-spanning mirror mimics the look
of a paned window and spreads sunlight
around a breakfast nook. The same
concept applies in nearly any room: Hang
a mirror at the end of a narrow hallway,
on a staircase landing or over a fireplace,
foyer table or dining room sideboard to
visually expand a space.

THE BIG BUY
SOFA

You wouldn't buy a new car without giving it a test drive or reading some reviews. The same goes for your sofa.

SECTIONAL

Best for: households of three or more who like to spread out (or snuggle up) to watch TV, play video games or read; also good for seating plenty of party guests. Just check that the couch isn't so large that it limits traffic flow through the room. And keep the back low—32 inches or less—so that it doesn't appear hulking. The chic **WEST ELM® PEGGY MID-CENTURY L-SHAPED SECTIONAL** fits the bill.

STANDARD

Best for: everyone else. A stylish standard sofa, like the **ROWE NOTTING HILL**, gives you more decorating flexibility. Flank it with comfy armchairs, pair it with a loveseat or use an upholstered storage bench as a coffee table—and you'll have plenty of seating for every day or special occasions.

COUCH-SHOPPING
CHECKLIST

- **Check the frame.** Soft wood, particleboard, plastic or metal frames may warp or wobble after five years. Hardwood is best. To test frame strength: Lift one front corner or leg of the sofa off the floor. By the time you've raised it 6 inches, the other front leg should have risen, too.

- **Ask about joinery.** What you want: wooden dowels, double wooden dowels, wooden corner blocks or metal screws and brackets.

- **Test the springs.** Sit down firmly on an outside edge of the sofa. Squeaks and creaks suggest that springs are incorrectly placed or hitting the frame.

- **Feel your fillings.** Two good cushion options: high-resilient (HR) foam in a layer of down and conventional foam wrapped in polyester batting. Top of the line? Goose down mixed with feathers.

- **Find tough textiles.** Tight-weave cotton is a winner. Also terrific: synthetic microfiber (it's stain resistant). Buyer beware: Blends of natural and synthetic fibers tend to pill.

SOFT TOUCHES

Want your rooms to say, "Come in and stay awhile"?
Layer on the fabric accents.

DRAPE YOURSELF IN STYLE

Beyond their intended purposes (e.g.,
controlling outdoor light, regulating
indoor temperatures and, you know,
providing a little privacy), floor-to-ceiling
drapes draw the eye up, which makes your
room seem taller. If your home gets a lot
of sunlight, select a fade-proof fabric like
Sunbrella® for your curtains.

ADD SOME PADDING

Are you and your partner on different ends of the how-many-pillows-should-be-on-the-bed spectrum? Compromise with an upholstered headboard. A rectangular or camelback style in a neutral hue offers classy cushiness, while one in a dramatic silhouette, color or pattern becomes a bold focal point.

SEAL ALL-STAR
JCPENNEY HOME™ EASY CARE SHEETS

When GH Institute tests textiles, it washes and dries every sheet five times—to check for shrinking, fading, wrinkling and other signs of wear. JCPenney's Home collection always does well. Plus, the sheets come in more than a dozen pretty hues and prints to fit any color scheme. Also notable by JCP: **The Liz Claiborne® 400tc Ultra Fine Cotton Sateen Sheet Set** is super-soft, resists pilling and holds up after multiple washings.

CREATE A READING NOOK

Turn unused space under a window into
a cozy seating area. Consider making
cushions or having them sewn to fit
window seats or other architectural nooks.
Add a cozy throw blanket and pillows.
Drawers below create extra storage.

CHANGE UP YOUR SHOWER CURTAIN

Go with a cheery color and one thing is guaranteed: Visitors will no longer fixate on the pink tile or low sink. Or do the opposite—create a spa-like blank slate with all-white textiles in various textures: shower curtain with decorative "ribbon" and matching towels, plus a nubby bath mat. Everyone now: *Ahh.*

PATTERN PLAY

Show some personality with prints. It's the decorating equivalent of letting your hair down.

ESTABLISH PRIORITIES

Let a bold wallpaper be the star of the show. Keep additional artwork sparse and simple: A small collection of gilded frames, for example, won't overpower the paper's design. Likewise, unfussy furniture—a clean-lined table, clear acrylic chairs—don't compete with your primary pattern.

KEEP YOUR BALANCE

The number one rule for layering patterns? Stay in the same color palette. Start with a wow-factor print that sets the tone, like a bold zigzag or a bright abstract. Find a fabric that echoes the colors in your main pattern but features smaller-scale prints. Add a stripe, a check or a solid, and you're officially a mix master!

GO SMALL

Not ready to commit to all-over prints? Not to worry. Even a dash of a vibrant repeat has major impact against a blank background—think orange or yellow chevron-patterned pillows on a white sofa. Another solution: Keep your patterns soft and neutral (e.g., gray and white, tan and cream) to add subtle visual texture.

CURATE YOUR COLLECTIONS

First, edit out those not-so-favorite things, then arrange
the keepers in style. You'll love them that much more.

BRIGHTEN WITH BOOKS

Bibliophiles, rejoice: Now your collection
of beloved hardcovers and yellowed
paperbacks can serve a second purpose—as
handy decorating tools. Simply group your
different genres by spine shade. The effect?
A hit of color as pretty as a painting.

INSPIRE THE SCHEME

Celebrate everyday objects like graphic-print plates—they'll stand out against basic, uncluttered bookshelves. While you're at it, why not use their colors throughout the room? Here, hardwood floors are stained a leafy green to match.

STRENGTH IN NUMBERS

Group different vases, candlesticks or other interesting objects in the same color family to achieve a sculptural effect. And employ this tried-and-true interior stylist's trick: Go with odd numbers of items—they tend to look more balanced than even ones.

CASH IN!
TURN OLD FURNITURE
INTO $$$

Sure, you could have a killer tag sale, but there are easier—and more profitable—ways to pocket some green.

On **CRAIGSLIST®** and **EBAY®**, brand names in like-new condition usually bring in bigger bucks (Pottery Barn® tables, KitchenAid mixers), but items from another era (e.g., china pieces produced from a limited run) are also in demand.

REPLACEMENTS, LTD.®, buys china, crystal and flatware from anywhere in the United States. Once you receive a quote, ship it to them: If they like what they see, they'll pay within a week; if they don't, they'll return it free of charge.

FACEBOOK® "yard sale" themed groups bring together buyers and sellers: Post a photo of the item for sale, and friends in your group will see it. Interested buyers contact you via the comments page or private message.

CHAIRISH is a stylish buy-and-sell site for design aficionados. But don't be discouraged if you don't have a spare Barcelona® chair to hawk. The site also accepts "non-branded items with great character." It's free to list, and you'll make 80 percent on any sale.

TOP-DOLLAR TRICK

Reveal what the item you're selling is going for at retail now—along with what you paid for it way back when. This may put the asking price in a better light.

UPCYCLE THE ORDINARY

Make your own patio table with
inexpensive wood pallets, some white
exterior paint plus heavy-duty metal
casters. Finish the look of the alfresco
living room with gauzy curtains and
paper lanterns.

GOOD
HOUSEKEEPING

TAKE IT OUTSIDE

LAYER ON LUSHNESS

The trick to enjoying your great outdoors more? Spending less time tending to it. Opt for native species and skip labor-intensive annuals. Here, undemanding perennials and flowering shrubs with long bloom cycles provide pops of color.

MADE FOR SHADE

A great outdoor umbrella lets you live outdoors all day and—in a bright color or chic stripe—makes a major style statement. When it comes to size, the umbrella's diameter should be at least 5 feet larger than the table (i.e., a 4-foot table needs a 9-foot spread).

CONTAIN YOUR ENTHUSIASM

Container gardening is a good first step for wannabe green thumbs. And some of the easiest plants to grow are succulents, which stow water in their stems and leaves and thrive in shallow vessels. In a clever front yard bird bath, pebbles help hold in moisture.

FRONT DOOR DO-OVERS

Like putting on a little makeup and jewelry, freshening up your entryway can make the difference between pretty and "pow!"

SERENE GREEN

A calming sage, this front door color complements a white exterior as well as the surrounding foliage.

TRADITIONAL TOUCHES

All in a row, footed planters holding topiary-style shrubs plus a decorative dog statue add to the stately vibe.

RED, BRIGHT AND BLUE

Blue is an American classic (especially against red brick!), but opting for bright cobalt instead of traditional navy looks anything but staid. Brass hardware stands out against this hue.

PLAYFUL IN PINK

Unexpected shades like peony pink are a great way to welcome guests into a fun-filled home. A playful brass fox knocker adds a touch of whimsy.

SEAL ALL-STAR
OLYMPIC ONE

A fresh coat of outdoor paint has a return on investment (ROI) that's one of the highest for a home project—it almost pays for itself come selling time. In evaluating Olympic® One®'s exterior flat line for the coveted Seal, the GH Institute experts confirmed that the two-in-one paint and primer delivered on its claims of providing all-climate protection and resisting cracking, peeling and fading. And yes, it comes in lots of gorgeous colors, too.

LOVE YOUR LANDSCAPING

Make the most of your yard with these expert tips.

CREATE AN ARBOR

Planting a tree by your entrance is so welcoming! Just make sure its leaves and roots won't cause future problems for your home's roof or foundation. The best time to prune it: the winter—the plant's architecture will be visible (in the case of deciduous trees) and insect and disease concerns are at a minimum (deciduous and evergreen trees).

MIND YOUR MULCH

When in doubt, pick organic mulch over inorganic (brick chips, shredded rubber)—it keeps the ground cool, holds in moisture, lets plant roots breathe and breaks down to enrich the soil. But skip free mulch, unless you know the source. If it contains weeds, mushrooms or diseased wood or plants, it can spread those scourges to your yard.

SHOW OFF YOUR HANDIWORK

Solar accent lights can illuminate your walkway or special landscaping features—and won't waste any electricity. On a path, place lamps close enough together that their light overlaps (typically every 3 to 6 feet).

THAT'S GENIUS! Fill an empty **Parmesan cheese shaker** with plant food as an easy way to feed flowerbeds or your garden.

DITCH THE GRASS

If keeping your lawn green has you seeing red, don't despair. Look into "no-mow" grass, which doesn't grow as tall, clover or a blend of the two. They cover large areas and need far less TLC. For the least maintenance of all, consider hardscaping: gravel, slate tiles or another rocklike ground cover—a smart solution in drought-prone areas.

CURE A SICK LAWN

The top four grass-related grumbles, solved.

BROWN SECTIONS It's tempting to set the mower blades low so you won't have to cut the lawn again so soon. But slicing off more than an inch of grass at a time can cause what remains to turn brown.

TRAMPLED PATHS If your family and guests are always trekking across the grass, take it as a cue that the route should be recognized. Install slate or concrete paving stones.

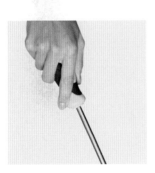

BRITTLE GRASS If blades look withered or snap easily, it may be that the ground's too dry. To test, push a screwdriver into the soil in a few spots. If it doesn't go in smoothly to a depth of six inches, haul out the hose.

OVERALL YELLOWING Surprise: Fertilizer may be causing your jaundiced lawn—the same nitrogen in it that causes it to grow can "burn" the grass if overdosed. After a treatment, water the yard well to dilute the fertilizer and help soak it down.

DIY PET URINE DETERRENTS

Your hydrangeas shouldn't double as a litter box. Combine **used coffee grounds and orange peels** to create a pungent mixture. Sprinkle it on top of your soil, and the neighbor's cat won't go near the odor.

As for those yellow urine patches, the only way to prevent them is to curb your dog. If you catch him (or another pup) lifting his leg on the grass, quickly **douse the spot with a hose.** Existing yellow patches may need reseeding.

Pet relieved himself *indoors*? Try this GH Institute method to get urine out of carpet: Mix 1 Tbsp. of liquid hand dishwashing detergent and 1 Tbsp. of white vinegar with 2 cups of warm water. Using a clean white cloth, sponge the stain with the solution. Blot until the liquid is absorbed. If the stain remains, use an eyedropper to apply hydrogen peroxide, and then add a drop or two of ammonia (not on silk or wool). Sponge with cold water and blot dry.

FUN NOT FUSSY

Mix up plant shapes and colors for an informal effect. Here a rustic stone path is bordered by sedum (Sedum), juniper (Juniperus) and castor oil plant.

PRETTY PLANTING IDEAS

Use your creativity in the garden to enhance Mother Nature's offerings.

CLIMB THE WALLS Liven up a plain patio wall with a sun-seeking climber like bougainvillea—the twining vertical vines balance the bushiness below.

STEP BY STEP Situate curvaceous containers on stairs and fill with a variety of shaped plants, from scallop-leafed geraniums to spiky agave.

EYE-CATCHING EDIBLES Gather potted herbs on a table to transform a small patch of porch. Or give an urban balcony a country vibe.

GARDEN VARIETY A mismatched mix of glazed graphic pots can add personality to a yard. Overturn some so that there's a subtle staggering of heights.

GREEN SCREEN

Covered with English ivy, a frill-free chain-link fence from the home-improvement store acts as a natural privacy barrier—starting at the front gate and snaking backward. Copy the idea to, say, shield a patio from view.

GOTTA HAVE 'EM!
GARDENING GO-TOS

These GH Institute–tested tools and innovations help you plant (and water!) your way to a bountiful yard. Dig in!

GARDENING GLOVES

Keep your hands clean and safe while you're working in the dirt. Gloves with a silicone grip like Bionic™'s let you pick up tiny clippings easily.

CUTE CLOGS

How to muck through mud without trekking clods into the house? Simple! Slip on a pair of comfy, easy-to-remove, clean-'em-with-the-hose garden clogs. Some come in lots of playful colors and patterns.

LIGHTWEIGHT WHEELBARROW

This is your ultimate sidekick for hauling gear or seedlings to your gardening spot, then hauling away cut branches, weeds and more. Save your back and opt for a heavy-duty plastic version. **JACKSON® PROFESSIONAL TOOLS EZ POUR™ SPOUT WHEELBARROW** has a narrow spout for easy mulching.

STURDY SPADE

This multipurpose tool takes some of the work out of weeding—yanking up ones with semi-deep roots as well as grass that's growing in the wrong place. Use it to bury bulbs for spring, too.

POWERFUL PRUNERS

Whether for your private Eden or a lone window box, you need a reliable trimmer—pruning makes plants prettier and helps them live longer. **FISKARS® POWERGEAR® BYPASS PRUNER** topped GH Institute tests.

SMART FEEDER

Now, fertilizing is as simple as turning on the water. The nifty **MIRACLE-GRO® LIQUAFEED® UNIVERSAL FEEDER** attaches right to an outdoor faucet.

OUTDOOR ROOMS

How to make your outside areas feel more inviting? Treat them like rooms of the house, and decorate accordingly.

PLOP ON PILLOWS

In the same way that accent pillows can cozy up a couch or jazz up a bed, fun weather-resistant cushions add personality and plushness to your outdoor seating.

PULL UP SOME SEATS

Expand a kitchen sill with an extra
countertop (turn to page 97 for one with
the GH Seal). Pull up sturdy stools for
diner-style eating on your deck.

MAKE A POSH OUTHOUSE

Keep dirty feet out of the house with the
ultimate washroom. To do: Enclose a space
with fencing; add a toilet, sink and shower;
then choose a few cute accessories.

GET DECKED OUT

Pretty up your porch: A good deck stain
seals out moisture, adds UV protection
and guards against wear. Plus,
today's formulas come in a range of
eye-pleasing hues (think pale gray,
sky blue or even coffee). Try
GH Seal holder Rust-Oleum
Restore® 10X Advanced.

QUALITY TESTED
GOOD
HOUSEKEEPING
Since ★ 1909
LIMITED WARRANTY · ghseal.com for details

CLEAR THE DECK!

Give your outdoor space a quick cleanup—without getting down and dirty.

1. **FIRST STEP:** Clear off the leaf litter. Move chairs out of the way and sweep debris to the ground.

2. **USING YOUR GARDEN HOSE** with a nozzle, give the wood, stone or concrete a blasting (go easy on broken spots), starting at the house end and working outward.

3. **WHILE YOU'RE AT IT**, spray surrounding greenery to minimize damage from soap runoff later.

4. **FOR PROBLEMATIC GREASE OR MILDEW STAINS**, sprinkle on a little laundry detergent—powder with bleach is best—and rub it in with your broom. After a few minutes, rinse.

STAYCATION ESSENTIALS

Reimagine your yard and turn every weekend into a family getaway.

OPEN YOUR OWN RESTAURANT

One with outdoor seating, naturally. Decorate with lanterns or string lights overhead and flowers on the table so even basic BBQ feels special. If regular rain or heavy sun is an ongoing concern, consider investing in a motorized awning to attach to your house. A good bet: SunSetter®'s styles have had the GH Seal since 1999.

ADD SOME AMBIANCE

Music makes everything better—even a ham on whole wheat out in the hammock! If you can't pipe your tunes from indoors to outdoors, and the iPhone®-in-a-bowl trick isn't cutting it, invest in a portable wireless speaker such as the GH Institute-reviewed Jawbone® Big Jambox®.

BUST OUT THE BAR

Stock your bar cart well—because you can't make fruit coolers without the proper ingredients and a fancy glass! A rolling bar lets you bring the fun with you, and you can put bottles, etc., away easily when you're done.

COMMANDEER THE KIDDIE POOL

Use it for your off-duty mom spa appointment (and, yes, you will take a glass of champagne, thank you). Or, you know, set it up for the kids. Turn on a beach-inspired Pandora® station, put on your sunglasses and chill out.

THE BIG BUY
OUTDOOR GRILL

When the GH Institute experts test grills, they do them just like you would: searing steaks and slow cooking chicken. Tough job, but someone's got to do it!

CONSIDER SIZE CAREFULLY

If you mostly grill for small crowds, consider buying a two- or three-burner model.

A four-burner grill is great if you entertain frequently and have large parties, but it's more expensive and uses more propane.

THE WINNER

Our top pick cooks up the best BBQ and has plenty of grill space (room for 28 burgers), a side burner for warming sauce, a fuel gauge and tons of storage below. Plus it comes in three colors. **WEBER® GENESIS® GAS GRILL EP-330** in green.

ONE FOR THE ROAD

This compact mini folds up for easy storage/ traveling yet can handle 16 big burgers and has two side tables. Hook it up to a one-pound tank; it turns on just like a gas range. **NAPOLEON TRAVELQ™ TQ285X-BL**.

STAINLESS STEAL

Perfect grill marks, no smoking or flare-ups, a side burner and space for 28 burgers... and reasonably priced. Note: "High" gets too hot to cook chicken. **NEXGRILL® 4-BURNER PROPANE GAS GRILL WITH SIDE BURNER 720-0830H**.

LAID-BACK AND LOVELY

Just because you're throwing a "garden" party doesn't mean you have to serve finger sandwiches (though that's totally fine, if that's what you want). Modernize the menu with grilled pizza and pasta salad, which can be enjoyed hot or cold.

chapter

7

GOOD
HOUSEKEEPING

EASY ENTERTAINING

HOST WITHOUT THE HASSLE

Try these savvy strategies to throw a soiree everyone will enjoy (including *you*).

PREP (WAY) AHEAD

To alleviate your hosting stress, make a schedule a few weeks beforehand and assign yourself manageable tasks each day. For instance, decorate weeks ahead and shop for groceries a couple of days in advance. The day before, start your chopping or baking, rearrange any furniture, set the table and stock the bathroom with TP.

HAVE TRASHY THOUGHTS

Consider how much mess your party might produce, and make disposal easier on yourself from the get-go. Allow at least one large garbage bag for every 10 people. Line trash bins with more than one bag so that you can simultaneously remove and replace. Likewise, place a recycling bin next to the drinks station so that people can drop in empties.

BEAT BUGS TO THE PUNCH

Talk about a buzzkill: when your backyard buffet—not to mention partygoers—is swarmed with flies, mosquitoes or other winged pests. Provide guests with bug repellant spray or wipes. But ditch the citronella candles. GH Institute evaluations show that lanterns with active agents like allethrin, geraniol and metofluthrin are more effective.

FRESHEN THE FEAST

At a self-service sort of shindig, you don't want perishable foods to sit out for more than two hours. Will dishes be outside in the summer heat? Cut that time in half. Use smaller serving bowls and don't top them off—bring out new dishes to replenish as needed. Outdoors, position your buffet under an overhang or umbrella.

THAT'S GENIUS! A blustery day won't ruin your outdoor party when **binder clips** stop the tablecloth from blowing away.

KNOW YOUR CROWD

For a typical party, plan for eight to ten hors d'oeuvres per person. And make sure main dishes are fork-only, if you expect that most partygoers will stand and mingle. However, don't assume everyone is fine with standing. If your fete is longer than two hours, have seats for 80 percent of the attendees.

GOTTA HAVE 'EM! PARTY PICKS

Add these items to your entertaining arsenal, and you'll be ready to celebrate at the drop of a (party) hat.

PRETTY PITCHER

Pour a specialty punch or plain old iced water in style with a shapely pitcher. Stock up on a couple, and you can use one to hold a flower arrangement for a brunch fete or flag favors for that Fourth of July block party.

DECORATIVE PAPER NAPKINS

Patterned or colorful disposable napkins make any get-together more fun, even if you use your everyday dinnerware. Plus, they're an inexpensive way to establish a party theme. Keep a few packs on hand to dress up drinks when guests drop by.

FLAMELESS CANDLE

Put it in the bathroom for a lovely flickering effect. While it may be tempting to use a real candle to add light or a nice scent, it's never a good idea to burn candles in rooms that are not constantly occupied, according to the GH Institute.

CARVING SET

The last thing you want to do is hack up that beautiful bird you just roasted. Slice into it smoothly with a sharp (and sharp-looking) stainless steel knife and fork set. Joseph Joseph®'s Duo™ Carve nestles neatly together thanks to magnets in each handle.

FOOD WARMER

Forget bulky chafing dishes. Separate compartments atop a warming tray give you many more serving options. Clear lids like those on this Bella® style server mean guests can see what's inside—and will be eager to sample your spread.

PETITE PLATTERS

Every party needs some sort of appetizers—from mixed nuts to shrimp cocktail to crostini. On small trays, the finger foods are easier to pass or place. Even better: If the platters nest, they'll take up less space when stored.

SIMPLY CHIC
PLACE SETTINGS

Set a table that'll impress your guests. Here's your inspiration!

BOHO BEAUTIFUL

Mix intricate prints in a similar color
family for a rich setting. Sleek-handled,
gilded flatware isn't too flashy or fussy.
Flight of fancy: a feather tucked into a
nametag.

CASUALLY COOL

The kids (and you!) are never too old for a playful place setting. This chalkboard-style name card picks up the burnished black of a bronze fork and knife. A grid-patterned tray makes a fun placemat.

TO DYE FOR

Perfect for Easter or other springtime events, try creating a place setting with ombré watercolor linens. All you need is fabric paint, a place to let linens dry overnight and an iron to set the color.

SEAL ALL-STAR
DIXIE ULTRA® PLATES

Sure, elegant place settings and fine china have their place. But sometimes you just don't want to have to do dishes after a get-together—particularly if it's a large buffet-style gathering or backyard bash. A longtime GH Seal holder, Dixie Ultra plates will support a feast, so guests can load up on your famous potato salad without the fear of soak-through or plate collapse.

SWEET TREATS

Try hosting a daytime buffet-style fete,
like a dessert bar. Party favors can
feature a standout sweet—say, macarons
or your famous peanut brittle. Nestle
them in gift boxes and embellish with
the honoree's initial.

RETHINK THE KEG

Impress your guests with this fresh idea:
Turn a watermelon into a cocktail keg.
Take a thin slice off the bottom of the
melon, cut off the top and scoop it out.
Carve a hole, attach a spigot, pour in some
rum punch—and let the fun begin!

RUSTIC MODERN

Create subtle layers: Take clean, classic white plates, slip in a curvy one, and then top with a white-painted pear name holder. Spruce it up with extra herbs like sage.

SET A FORMAL TABLE

Why the strict blueprint? It follows the logical progression of the meal, and makes dining more comfortable for guests. How to get it right:

STACK IN STYLE Each place setting should have a dinner plate or liner plate (a "charger"). On top of that, place your salad plate, followed with a folded napkin.

DESSERT FORK AND SPOON Lots of settings? Tuck in dessert utensils above the plate—fork handle left, spoon handle right.

GLASSES Water is placed above knives for easy access. If you're serving both red and white wine, set glasses right to left in the order used.

UTENSILS Forks on the left; knives (blades in) and spoons on the right. Everything is placed from the outside in based on course order (e.g., set for soup, salad and then entrée).

15-MINUTE CENTERPIECES

Decorate quickly for any occasion with these crafty creations
featuring flowers, produce and two different kinds of shells.

BLOSSOM FOURTH

All-white flowers like hydrangeas seem
instantly all-American presented in a vase
that evokes the stars and stripes. Measure
the vase's circumference, then cut lengths
of patriotic ribbon to size. Attach with
double-sided tape to cover the vase.

FLOAT YOUR FLOWERS

If your long-stem roses or backyard blossoms are looking a little limp, give them a break—and snip off the flowers just below the head. Float them in a large bowl in the center of the table, or one flower per vessel in a grouping or row.

LINE 'EM UP

Seasonal simplicity doesn't get any
easier than this streamlined display.
Just parade small white pumpkins along
a wooden platter, and—to play up the
gourds' paleness—add a runner or fabric
remnant in autumnal orange.

SEE SHELLS

Look no further than coastal surroundings for centerpiece-worthy supplies—think shells, driftwood or greens. Display in sea glass–inspired vessels, and use them to set the stage for a beachy bash. Even better: Set them on a distressed-board table, reminiscent of wooden boats and the sea.

HERBAL ESSENCE

For an understated winter table, embellish glass candleholders with fragrant dried bay leaves. Starting with the larger leaves, dab glue to the back, then attach them vertically to the votive holder (making sure leaves are a safe distance from the flame). Scent-sational!

CUT THE BEV BUDGET

For a typical party, plan on one and a half drinks per person per hour. Serve a pre-mixed drink, such as sangria or eggnog, which you can prepare beforehand (make several batches and bring out one at a time). Not only will you make guests feel special, you'll save money on liquor.

TRIM PARTY EXPENSES

Set a budget. Not having one is like going to the grocery store
on an empty stomach—you'll buy everything in sight.

TIME IT RIGHT Throw an appetizers-only party from 5 p.m. to right after sunset, for example. Or, if it's a child's birthday party, host it during the afternoon (after lunch but before dinner) and just serve cake. The kids will love you.

USE DIGITAL INVITES It's true—the world has gone digital, which means that even the way we plan our parties has changed. Save money on paper invitations by using free online services, like Paperless Post® or Evite®.

MAKE YOUR OWN MUSIC Set the right mood for your gathering with a well-managed (and inexpensive!) playlist by digital song sources, such as Spotify®, Pandora and Rdio®.

OPT FOR ONE-POT DISHES If you're serving a meal at your party, choose a one-pot dish. And consider making it a pasta, rice or potato recipe, or even a hearty salad. These can go a long way and often cost next to nothing.

STAY AWHILE

Before visitors arrive, hang out in their assigned room or area for an evening to see what is and isn't working. Lamp need a new bulb? Crumbs under the sleeper-sofa cushions? Cobwebs in the guest room ceiling corners? And don't forget the necessities: clean sheets, blankets, pillows, water glass (plus carafe, if possible) and an alarm clock.

READY THE GUEST ROOM

First, clear clutter in the area where guests will sleep, even if it's in the living room. The goal: Give lodgers space to get comfy—with landing spots for shoes, jewelry and more.

RACK IT UP Rather than emptying out drawers in a bureau, pick up inexpensive luggage racks so that an overnight guest doesn't have to unpack and can easily access clothes.

BATHROOM BASICS The unofficial houseguest's bill of rights should include a fresh towel and washcloth, tissues and plenty of TP (*without* having to hunt for it).

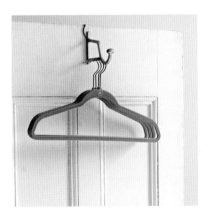

GIVE 'EM THE HOOK Don't want visitors to see what's lurking inside the closet? Hide it from scrutiny with an over-the-door hook and hangers.

PLAY TOUR GUIDE Keep area maps, transit schedules and brochures of local attractions in a conveniently placed folder for out-of-towners.

HAPPIER HOLIDAYS

'Tis the season for hosting family and friends. But how do you do it graciously without burning out? Try these clever cheats.

PRESENT PANTRY

Stock up early on last-minute gifts (candles, gift cards, wine) as well as wrapping materials. Stash them in an easy-access spot like the laundry room, so you can save face if a neighbor stops by with a treat (even better: have a couple of items wrapped already).

QUICK COVER

Disguise (and—voilà!—decorate) a sad-looking side table with a seasonal throw blanket. Employ the same camouflaging trick on any stained upholstered pieces.

EIGHT DAYS OF AWESOME

Need a new menorah? Okay, *want* a new menorah? Use glass votives and colored stones to DIY an elegant, unique Hanukkah candelabra for less.

FAMILY MATTERS

When you're having over more than a few people, you don't want your four-legged family member to become overwhelmed and act out of character (translation: freak out). So you'll want to plan ahead for pets. Also, some guests may have allergies. Instead of locking your dog or cat in a room (and potentially frightening them), consider hiring a pet sitter for the night. And make sure you vacuum well.

mix an orchid with ornaments!

KEEP IT SIMPLE

During the busy holiday season, an orchid is a wise floral choice—it requires almost no care and lasts for months! Buy colorful glass ornaments in bulk to spread Christmas cheer—on an evergreen garland, in a wreath or in glass vases or bowls.

INVITING AROMAS

Pop some cinnamon sticks into a
crackling fire to instantly perfume the air
and make the house smell festive. Extra
cooking ingredients work as potpourri
in a pinch: Place bowls of sliced citrus
fruits, or apples and spices like cloves and
cinnamon around your rooms.

THE BIG BUY
ARTIFICIAL CHRISTMAS TREE

Beyond aesthetic preference—whether you like a fluffy blue spruce, the ever-popular fir or a mid-century mod white tree—your options are primarily price-based.

$500 AND UP

For families who want to invest in a fully fuss-free Tannenbaum, most of today's artificial trees come pre-lit, which is a major time-saver. At $899, the GH Seal holder **7.5' BALSAM HILL® BH BALSAM FIR**'S true green color and the natural-looking fall of its branches helped it earn top marks in GH Institute tests. Plus, it has nice extras: an electrical connection for tree toppers, a foot-pedal on-off switch for the lights, as well as two zip-up bags for storing the tree in the off-season.

UNDER $500

For folks wanting a similar look for less, GH Institute panelists loved the "beautiful" plentiful lighting on the **GE 7.5' JUST CUT FRASER FIR**. Like the more expensive Balsam Hill, this fir has a foot-pedal on-off switch to easily control lights and an electrical connection for your angel or star. You're on your own for storage, though. At less than $300, it's hard to top.

REAL VS. FAKE

Maybe you're a purist and only want a fresh, piney evergreen, or perhaps you prefer traveling as far as your attic when it comes to decorating for Christmas. Here's how each type of tree treats the environment.

REAL

Chopping down the real thing isn't as harmful as you might think. Producing an artificial tree takes about eight times the energy of growing a live one. That said, skip the gas-guzzling trip to some wooded wonderland and buy local. When it's time to toss it, compost the tree or ask your town's waste authority for eco-friendly disposal options.

FAKE

An artificial tree can have less of an environmental impact, but there's a contingency clause: You have to keep it for a minimum of two years—ideally up to nine. Gotta toss it sooner? Avoid the landfill and donate gently used trees to the Salvation Army®, Goodwill® or another charity instead.

PREVENT THE SPREAD

Of the party, that is. Keep doors locked
or spaces decoratively blocked off to
discourage company from wandering.
Otherwise, you'll spend all night hunting
down half-empty wine glasses and dirty
dishes. Don't clean up too much during
the party, though—it can make guests feel
uncomfortable. *Do* help them help you:
Place an empty tray on a table so that
people can leave their dirty dishes all in
one spot.

FAST AFTER-THE-FEAST CLEANUP

Once guests go home, it's just you—and the mess.
Use these speedy tips for less work tomorrow.

CLEAR THE DINING TABLE Take any remaining dishes and utensils into the kitchen. Gather up the tablecloth or cloths, and shake crumbs over the kitchen sink or garbage can, or open up the back door and toss the crumbs in the yard.

WASH YOUR TABLE LINENS Fill the washing machine with warm water, add detergent and leave the items to soak overnight (newer machines may have an extended presoak setting). See any stains (e.g., red wine, gravy)? Pretreat before soaking. Finish the cycle in the morning.

DEAL WITH LEFTOVERS Food that you would normally refrigerate shouldn't sit out at room temperature for more than a couple of hours. Toss anything that's been out longer. Cover leftovers with foil or plastic wrap before refrigerating.

CONQUER COUNTERS Last, tackle what's left in and around the sink and not going into the dishwasher. Squirt grimy pots and pans with dishwashing liquid, and fill with very hot water. Set them aside on the counter or cooktop overnight.

FIX A WINDOW JAM

Paint that has worked its way between the sash and the jamb is often the culprit. Run the blade of a sharp utility knife around the edges of the sash to loosen any paint bonds. If that fails, try holding a small block of wood against the sash and tap it with a hammer. Repeat at intervals around all sides.

GOOD HOUSEKEEPING

FIX STUFF & SAVE MONEY

PROTECT YOUR PEEPERS

Almost 45 percent of eye injuries happen
at home. So, while you may feel silly
wearing safety goggles for your weekend
projects—using a power tool, mowing the
lawn or even just hammering in a nail—it's
always a good idea.

UPDATE WITH PAINT

Give cabinets a fresh new look without breaking the bank. What will do it: a happy hit of color inside like the orange in interior designer Kyle Schuneman's Los Angeles kitchen. Use a semigloss paint to ensure that shelves will be easy to wipe clean.

LITTLE FIXES, BIG RESULTS

You can do all of these DIY home repairs in minutes.
Then, pat yourself on the back. Or have a glass of wine.

UNSTICK THAT PESKY INTERIOR DOOR

First, tighten each screw in the hinges with a screwdriver (or replace them with larger-gauge screws, if they turn without tightening). Door still won't close? Swelling may be the issue. Smooth the edges where they hit the frame with coarse (60-grit) sandpaper. Open and close door.

MAKE THE TOILET STOP RUNNING

Stop jiggling the handle and start looking under the hood. The guilty party is likely a worn rubber flapper valve (which controls water going from tank to toilet), a loose or too-tight chain that prevents the flapper from closing completely *or* a jammed sliding mechanism or float ball. Pick up a new flapper for less than $10 or a full toilet-repair kit for about $20 at a home improvement store. GH Institute tip: Be sure to turn off the water supply before you start this repair.

ERASE MOLD SPOTS ON THE WALL

Clearly, you don't want to ignore them because you could develop allergies or other health problems. Here is how to proceed: Remove the fungi with a mixture of 1 cup of bleach and 1 gallon of warm water. Scrub the area thoroughly, then rinse with clean water (see the tip below, if splattering is a concern). When the spot is dry, repaint with a mildew-resistant latex paint. If it's a large mold infestation, or if it comes back, call in a pro.

THAT'S GENIUS! An **old plastic shower liner** makes a great drop cloth or protective cover for messy work, from drilling holes to dusting ceiling fan blades.

FILL CRACKS IN THE DRIVEWAY

Why care? The cracks will get bigger and
harder to repair. If they're near the house,
moisture may seep into the foundation.
To fix: Spray off loose debris with your
garden hose. Apply a crack filler designed
for asphalt and let it dry thoroughly.

GOTTA HAVE 'EM! TOP TOOLS

With these handy helpers in your kit, you'll be ready for almost any home repair or improvement.

CLAW HAMMER

GH Institute recommends a wood-handled "rip" claw style instead of a "framing" hammer. It should feel good in your grip and be lightweight enough to use easily, but not so light that it doesn't give you any force.

SUPER-STRONG GLUE

Poor Humpty Dumpty. If only all of the king's men had had **GORILLA® SUPER GLUE**! This Good Housekeeping Seal holder bonds metal, stone, wood, ceramics, foam, glass and much more.

DUCT TAPE

So durable, this waterproof tape can seal or stick to just about anything. People have even started using it to create crafts and clothes (Google it!). A nifty trick: Try it to lift sticker adhesive off glass. Rub it over the spot a few times, and peel the mess away.

TAPE MEASURE

Why you need it: to measure everything *twice*, as the adage goes. Use it when hanging pictures, installing shelves or even doing sewing projects. And definitely use it when you're going furniture or organizing bin shopping—to ensure your buys fit your footage.

COMFY SCREWDRIVER

For the best grip for women, check out **BLACK & DECKER'S SMARTDRIVER** cordless screwdrivers. The compact handle makes it easy to maneuver in tight spaces—perfect for repairing a loose drawer handle or assembling that new bookshelf.

HANDY DRILLS

For a lightweight option for smaller projects, the GH Institute loved the **12V BOSCH ⅜" DRILL DRIVER**. Need more power? Opt for the **CRAFTSMAN® 19.2V C3 ¼" HEAVY DUTY DRILL**.

SAVE ENERGY (AND MONEY!)

From changing your windows to changing your habits, these green ideas will help you conserve more green in your wallet.

REPLACE YOUR WINDOWS

Want to make your house more efficient *and* boost its value? Look no further than your windows. GH has three Seal holders—Window World™, Champion® and Earthwise Windows®—that can help. Most of their styles (e.g., double-hung, awning, casement, bay or bow) are Energy Star certified.

DOES IT PAY TO HIRE A PRO?

TO DO AN ENERGY AUDIT

Surprise! Many power companies offer these for *free*. In the New York area, for example, power provider ConEdison® will even help you install its recommendations—from lighting to appliances—and pay as much as 70 percent directly to the contractor. Even if you do have to fork out for a professional audit, it's usually worth it—particularly if you have a "leaky home," as the Department of Energy dubs an inefficient house. Find out more at energy.gov.

There's another reason to make "qualified efficiency updates" on your home. The US Congress has renewed the previously expired Residential Energy Efficiency Tax Credit and extended the Residential Renewable Energy Tax Credit for solar energy systems, so any updates you make in 2016 will be eligible for tax credits in 2017.

RECONSIDER YOUR HEATING NEEDS

Heating and cooling accounts for half of the energy used in your home. Start spending less by lowering your water heater's temperature. Most houses don't need water hotter than 120 degrees, and you can save up to $30 a year with each 10-degree reduction. Also, consider whether it's time to get rid of your old water heater, furnace or air conditioner. If the equipment is more than 10 years old, you could earn back $115 a year.

BEWARE PHANTOM POWER

Even when some electronics are turned off (like TVs, DVRs and computers), they may still consume "phantom" energy if plugged into an outlet, which can add up to $100 per year. How to avoid it: Unplug your devices when you're not using them, or use a power strip and cut off the juice with a flip of a switch.

TURN OLD ELECTRONICS INTO $$$

With new gotta-have-it upgrades coming out practically every year, technology depreciates *fast,* so if you're unloading old gadgets, try to do so quickly.

APPLE®'s Reuse and Recycling program gives you an Apple gift card for your iPad®, iPhone or Mac®. RadioShack® and other retailers also offer a trade-in program.

GAZELLE, a site that buys used devices, pays cash or offers an Amazon gift card for computers, smartphones and more. Plus, you have 30 days to get a new phone before mailing in your old one.

GLYDE calculates the true resale value or market price of your electronics and suggests a price, which may translate into a better deal. Once your game, tablet or phone is listed, Glyde users can take a look and, maybe, snatch it up.

EXCHANGEMYPHONE will give you an instant price quote for your phone. Take your payment via check or PayPal® deposit, or donate it to the numerous nonprofits listed on the site to get a tax credit.

TOP-DOLLAR TRICK

Selling a video game? Think about throwing in a console, even if it's older, to really up the price. Recently in demand: vintage models of gaming systems, such as Nintendo®, Xbox® or PlayStation®.

everything on
this table $3

books
$1

TAG SALE TIPS

Choose a good moneymaking day, such
as a Saturday near the first or 15th of the
month (typical paydays). Then, arrange
wares for easy browsing: Group same-
priced items (e.g., books, $1) with a single
sign, and use office-supply stickers for
larger items. If things don't sell quickly,
lower prices. You want to off-load this
stuff, right?

BEST. YARD SALE. EVER.

Hosting a tag sale can be even better than picking through one, thanks to the extra cash and space you'll gain.

SIGN UP Place posters at key intersections near your street, or hang flyers with tear-off info in public spaces like your church or grocery store. (Before posting, consult area rules and ordinances.) Also put your sale on Craigslist or local newspapers and radio stations, if free.

MAXIMIZE YOUR EFFORTS Join with neighbors to have several sales on one street or combine wares at one location. For the latter, assign each family different colored price stickers; stick tags on a tally sheet as items sell. Stock a money box or bag with enough change.

TRY ONE ON Rather than dumping clothes and accessories in a box, display them. Hang items from a clothesline or a coat rack, and prevent jewelry tangles by stowing baubles in a muffin tin. Place a mirror nearby so that buyers can check themselves out.

GRAB BAGS Collect shopping bags and newspapers leading up to the sale. You'll be set to package fragile purchases. Planning to sell large or heavy items? Have the number of a local mover on hand, in case buyers can't cart away things themselves.

BEFORE YOU BUY

The most important thing to ask before you buy a connected home device: "Is my Internet fast enough?" Without a reliable connection, you are going to run into problems. The FCC recommends a minimum download speed of 4 megabits per second for adequate HD movie streaming and video conferencing. However, you'll need that number to be higher if you're connecting a lot of devices. Sites such as speedof.me or speedtest.net can help you test.

SMARTIFY YOUR HOME

Imagine it: You're headed home and, with a few taps on your smartphone, you preheat the oven, tweak the thermostat, turn on the porch light and start a load of laundry. Sound futuristic? It's not—with these GH Institute–tested devices.

CUSTOMIZABLE LIGHTING These bulbs can change color, turn on and off and send you alerts with just one swipe on an app. A breeze to install and set up, the **PHILIPS® HUE STARTER KIT** (3 bulbs and a hub) is fun and functional—you can set the lights on timers *and* upload a photo to match its color. So cool!

SMART THERMOSTAT Save cash by controlling your home's heating and cooling from wherever you are. The sleek **NEST®** thermostat starts learning your habits in just a few days, and also relies on local weather forecasts to help set your home's temperature.

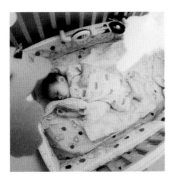

REMOTE VIDEO ACCESS The latest "nanny cams" come with tons of cool features, all of which you can manage remotely. Ideal for eyeballing your baby in his crib, the **D-LINK® WI-FI BABY CAMERA** has awesome video quality and a focused field of view. It even senses motion and sounds to alert you when your little one is waking.

GARAGE DOOR OPENER Never accidentally leave it open again! If your connectivity is reliable (read: no Wi-Fi dead spots in the garage) and you've got a great handyman for installation, consider a controller like the **GOGOGATE®**. It operates up to three garage doors wirelessly from your smartphone, when linked with your switch or ceiling motor.

DRIVE DOWN CAR COSTS

Want to save up to 20 percent or more on the cost of gas?
Follow these simple strategies.

TUNE UP

Whether it's a clogged air filter, poor
alignment or tires in need of air, any
number of "little" problems could
be dragging down your vehicle's
performance—and costing you money at
the pump. Some perspective: A clean air
filter can improve gas mileage by as much
as 10 percent, while a properly maintained
engine can save you up to 4 percent.

SLOW DOWN

For every 5 miles per hour you lower your highway speed, you can reduce fuel consumption by 7 percent. While you're at it, avoid jackrabbit starts and stops. Herky-jerky highway driving adds as much as one-third to your gas bill.

LIGHTEN YOUR LOAD

Why you shouldn't drive around with too much junk in the trunk: Your vehicle loses 1 to 10 percent in fuel efficiency for every 100 extra pounds it carries around. That works out to about 3 cents per gallon. Not nothing!

EMERGENCY PREP

From blackouts to big storms, here's how to weather these stressful situations—and keep your family safe.

THE BASICS

Every second counts in a true emergency. So corral the following in a portable container in the area of the house where you'll seek shelter, yet within easy reach for evacuation: three days' worth of food and water, a first aid kit, battery-powered (or hand-crank) flashlights and radio, batteries (if needed), trash bags and duct tape (for sheltering in place) plus any personal sanitation or specific family needs, like pet supplies.

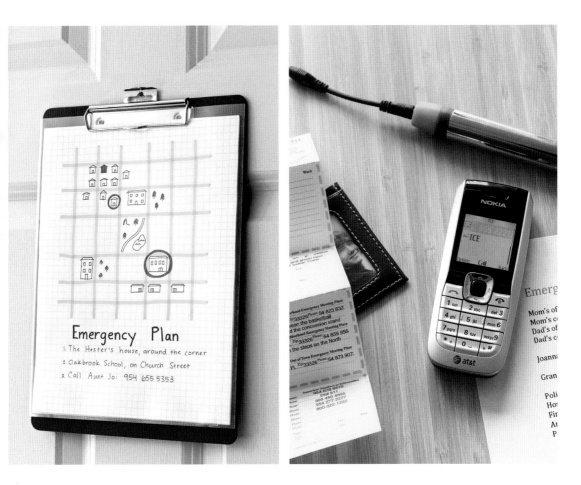

THE MEET UP

Designate two family meeting places (nearby and farther away in your neighborhood). Hang the plan near your kit; review it annually.

THE LIST

When disaster strikes, don't rely on memory or technology—save important digits on mini contact lists (ready.gov has templates you can print out) in family members' wallets and in your emergency kit.

THE WORK KIT

Be prepared anywhere: Keep a kit at your workplace stocked with comfortable shoes (if you won't be able to walk a distance in your usual ones), snacks, water and a flashlight. And know your company's emergency procedures. In general, have on hand enough cash for five days of basic needs (gas, food)—but even $20 will help if ATMs are down.

THE BIG BUY
GENERATOR

It may not seem like a necessity, but you'll be more than thankful
to have a generator when power outages strike. Read on
before the next blizzard or lightning bolt hits.

PERMANENT

Best for: ease of use. Permanent standby
generators turn on automatically, and
there's no need to hook up appliances.
Ones like those by GH Institute-evaluated
GENERAC* may run you around $1,900
to $5,000-plus and require professional
installation (which can cost as much as the
generator itself). *But,* under truly extreme
circumstances, a reliable standby
generator is worth the investment—to
prevent both major discomfort (to your
family) and damage (to your home).

PORTABLE

Best for: powering the basics without
spending a bundle. You can set up a
portable model by yourself for around
$1,000. (That said, budget for gasoline
or propane to fuel it, too—typical
gasoline usage is 7 gallons for 10 hours.)
You can find a portable model
at home improvement stores like Home
Depot*, which carries both Generac and
BRIGGS AND STRATTON* brands.

SEAL ALL-STAR
GAF ROOFING*

Given that installing a new roof is such a large financial commitment,
it only makes sense (dollars and *cents*) to go with a company that has
earned the GH Seal year after year. GAF Roofing offers nearly all of the
essential supplies. And rest assured: The shingles come in numerous
styles and can do anything from reflecting sunlight to conserving attic
heat to withstanding high winds.

PHOTO CREDITS

Cover: © Brian Woodcock; back cover, clockwise from top: Mike Garten; © Kate Mathis; © Victoria Pearson; spine: Shutterstock: © KonstantinChristian; © Antonis Achilleos: **33** (bookshelf); © Lucas Allen: iv, **81**, **180**; courtesy of Anna Sigga, www.scrappalicious.com: **47**; courtesy of Anolon: **89**; © Courtney Apple: iv, **24**, **122**; © Michel Arnaud: **97** (Cesarstone); © Burcu Avsar: **41** (tiered lazy susan); Jesus Ayala/ Studio D: **69** (jeans); © James Baigrie: **7**; Chris Bain: **59** (Tide and Oxiclean); © Christopher Baker: **167** (candles); courtesy of Balsam Hill: **157**; © Stacy Bass: **111** (orange room); courtesy of BELLA Housewares: **157**; courtesy of Bella Storage Solution: **41**; courtesy of Benjamin Moore: **134**; © Ryan Benyi: **61**; courtesy of Bionic Gloves: **143**; courtesy of Bissell Homecare, Inc.: **11** (Little Green steamer); courtesy of BLACK+DECKER, Inc.: **187**; courtesy of Robert Bosch Tool Corporation: **187**; © Stacey Brandford: **97** (x2), **98**, **104**, **106**, **125**; courtesy of Briggs & Stratton: **201**; © Liz Clayman Photography: iv, **76**; courtesy of ClosetMaid: **68**; courtesy of The Container Store: **53** (3 bin hamper), **66**, **73** (shoe boxes); Corbis: © Tetra Images: **70**; Depositphotos: © Dessie_bg: **71** (vacuum sealed bag); © Ha4ipiri: **73** (clip hanger); © kitchbain: **95** (gloves); maxxyustas: **55**; © Miki Duisterhof: **121**; courtesy of Eau Palm Beach Resort and Spa: **119**; Chris Eckert/Studio D: **113** (paint liner); courtesy of Electrolux: **21**, **55**; © Don Freeman: **26**; Philip Freidman/Studio D: **41** (ottoman), **45** (hangers), **62**, **71** (cedar), **86**, **87** (food processor, pressure cooker), **89** (hand blender), **95** (vinegar), **113** (tape, brush), **143** (wheelbarrow), **185** (shower curtain); courtesy of Frigidaire: **93**; courtesy of GAF: **201**; © Dana Gallagher: **17** (living room), **31**, **34**; Mike Garten: ii, **59**, **63**, **69** (boots), **80**, **89** (containers), **109**, **111** (magenta room), **159** (hand dyed), **161**; courtesy of Generac Power Systems: **201**; Getty Images: © Colin Anderson: **12**; © BanksPhotos: **150**; © Alistair Berg: **19**; © carlosalvarez: **89** (tongs); ©

ClarkandCompany: **196**; © davidfranklin/ Vetta: **154**; © Miki Duisterhof: **176**; © Edoneil: **141** (table); © Ron Evans: **138**; © Lus Ferraz/ EyeEm: **94**; © Fotografia Inc.: **17** (rug), **132**; © Fotosearch: **146**; © Fuse: **23** (sponge); © Mike Harrington: **16**; © Alex Hayden: **20**; © Hero Images: **22**, **194** (girl); © Paula Hible/FoodPix: **10**; © ingwervanille: **165**; © Junos: **37** (shredded paper); © Jupiterimages: **112**; © Mark Lund: **67**, **163** (blue table); © Joe McBride: **195** (baby); © missPiggy: **143** (clogs); © mollypix: **95** (towel); © Lauri Petterson: **179** (linens); © Victoria Pearson: **149**; © Terry Roberts Photography: **141** (steps); © Lisa Romerein: **133**; © Melissa Ross: **185** (tub); © Jeremy Samuelson: **58**; © Howard Shooter: **53** (laundry baskets); © Arthur Tilley: **135** (pink door); ©Mark Turner: **140**; © Dominique Vorillon: **141** (potted plants); © Jonelle Weaver: **141** (bougainvillea); © Barry Winiker: **135** (blue door); © Angela Wyatt: **6**; ©YinYang: **139** (stone walkway); © Tria Giovan: **120**; Ben Goldstein/Studio D: **37** (Fellowes), **113** (paint roller), **127** (KitchenAid), **143** (shears, smart feeder), **187** (hammer); Alison Gootee/Studio D: **75** (necklaces), **158**, **159**, **162**; courtesy of Gorilla: **187**; courtesy of Guardsman: **9**; © Alec Hemer: **145**; © Lisa Hubbard: **142**; © Jonas Ingerstedt: iv, **128**; iStock: © 101cats: **173** (dog); © Acerebel: **65** (emery board); © adlifemarketing: **23** (mop); © AnikaSalsera: **147** (deck), **179** (sink); © antoniotruzzi: **87** (pasta pot); © blackwaterimages: **187**(duct tape); © Ryhor Bruyeu: **137** (lit path); © cherezoff: **139** (screwdriver); © ChristopherBernard: **147** (leaves); © cisgraphics: **197** (packed car); © Anne Clark: **17** (kitchen); © constantgardener: **188**; © davidoff777: **91** (berries); © DmitriMaruta: **23** (vacuum); © Floortje: **91** (bread); © Fotoplanner: **89** (spatula); © duckycards: **191** (iPad); © gavran333: **88** (notebook); © Lorand Gelner: **178**; © John Gollop: **65** (floss); © IPGGutenbergUKLtd: **85** (groceries); © Izabela Habur: **71** (folding); © JazzIRT: **14**; © JestersCap: **17** (bathroom); © juanmonino: **87** (grill pan); © jwblinn: **95** (glass); © karamysh:

INDEX

HEARSTBOOKS

An Imprint of Sterling Publishing Co., Inc.
1166 Avenue of the Americas
New York, NY 10036

ISBN 978-1-61837-169-0

Distributed in Canada by Sterling Publishing Co., Inc.
c/o Canadian Manda Group, 664 Annette Street
Toronto, Ontario, Canada M6S 2C8

For information about custom editions, special sales, and premium and corporate purchases, please contact Sterling Special Sales at 800-805-5489 or specialsales@sterlingpublishing.com.

Manufactured in China

2 4 6 8 10 9 7 5 3 1

www.sterlingpublishing.com

Design and production: Susan Welt for gonzalez defino, ny

Good Housekeeping
Jane Francisco
Editor in Chief

Melissa Geurts
Creative Director

Good Housekeeping Institute
Laurie Jennings
Deputy Director, Editorial & Strategy

Rachel Rothman
Chief Technologist

Carolyn E. Forté
Director, Home Appliances, Cleaning Products & Textiles Lab

Sharon Franke
Director, Kitchen Appliances & Technology Lab